SCAT!

VOCAL IMPROVISATION
TECHNIQUES

BOB STOLOFF

**GERARD AND SARZIN
PUBLISHING CO.**

BROOKLYN, NEW YORK

CW01461202

Book Design by Charley Gerard
Forward and Introduction by Evan Sarzin

Copyright © 1996 by Bob Stoloff

All rights reserved. No part of this book may be reproduced or
transmitted in any form or by any means, electronic or mechanical,
including photocopying, recording, or by information storage and
retrieval system, without written permission of the publisher.

Gerard & Sarzin Publishing Co.
146 Bergen Street
Brooklyn, N.Y. 11217

Printed in the United States of America
ISBN 0-9628467-5-9 $25 softcover

Contents

Foreword

This book is the product of the ingenuity and skill of Bob Stoloff, a master of instru-vocalization and scat. It is also the fruit of our collaboration and friendship, which has thrived over the course of thirty-five years, with a minor two-decade interruption.

Bob was nine and I was seven when my family moved to the neighborhood. He was a witty, energetic boy with the facility of reproducing almost any sound with astonishing speed and articulation. At ten, Bob started in earnest on the trumpet after a brief and unhappy encounter with the violin. A year or so later, Bob sat down at his father's drum set one day and has never relinquished the sticks.

Bob and I became immediate and inseparable friends. Like an older brother, Bob blazed the trails. He led me into the world of TV wrestling, monster movies and girls. He led me gullibly on a wild goose-chase of a hunt for Captain Morgan's gold which just happened to be buried in my backyard. And of course, I followed his path into music. Dutifully, at ten I began to study the trumpet but lacked Bob's dedication and talent. Bob had discovered jazz, and he gave my first jazz albums to me. Not much happened at the time but the seeds were sown.

In 1969, when Bob was fifteen, his family moved away. I had to endure my high school years without the "tormentoring" of my older brother. After a few years of sporadic visits and conversations, we lost contact. From time to time, at concerts I was positive that I had spotted Bob in the trumpet section, finding that I had mistaken someone else for him. Although I had no idea where he was, I always assumed that Bob was making music.

Eventually, I swapped the trumpet for the sax, giving the term, "self-taught," a new and infamous meaning. This time it was my choice, however, and I genuinely embraced music for myself. By design or default, I went to college and law school while music remained my passion. Music did not unfold for me as it did for Bob. Those who can, do. Those who can't, write essays and conduct depositions.

After Gerard and Sarzin released Thelonious Monk: Originals and Standards, in 1991, I stumbled across a listing of Bob's books while thumbing through Jamey Aebersold's catalog.

In addition to sending copies of the books, Jamey was kind enough to give me Bob's address. I wrote to Bob and sent him a copy of our book. As abruptly as we had parted, we picked up without dropping a beat. I did not know how much we had missed until I recognized the mischievous glint in his eyes.

Bob is a man of dazzling ability, loyalty, heart and sincerity. He is a virtuoso, at one with his art. He is a gifted and generous teacher. And he is the brother I never had but never lost.

Evan Sarzin

After the recent death of Ella Fitzgerald, her presence hovers nearby, vivid and haunting. With a lifetime of brilliant work now complete, her legacy towers above all jazz singers due to the breadth and depth of her work. This book is dedicated to her spirit and her memory.

A History of Scat and Jazz Vocal Improvisation

Satchmo and the Origin of Scat

Does the singer imitate the instrument or voice versa? If you believe anecdotes, scat began when Louis Armstrong accidentally dropped his lyric sheet to "Heebie Jeebies" during a recording session and, thinking quickly, wordlessly sang the rest of the tune as if he were playing it. But what resulted was not a pure trumpet line. Although the young Armstrong's high baritone register was comparable to the limber, higher range of the trumpet, caught empty-handed, Satchmo filled the lines with syllables of speech. As the story goes, someone called it "scat," perhaps descriptive of one of the phrases— "Scat-a-lee-dat." Armstrong, affectionately known as Pops, established a career as a singer and a trumpeter. On vocals, Armstrong mixed the lyrics with trumpet-like scat obbligatos. Occasionally, though, he threw in an entire scat chorus. Armstrong's scat licks could be comical, sexy bawdy or poignant, and as a result many of these takes originally were unreleased.

There are no eyewitness accounts of this serendipitous moment, but the Armstrong creation myth has taken hold. Certainly, Armstrong was the first to record scat vocals, and he deserves credit for making it an art form. Satchmo was not the first musician to substitute syllables for lyrics or the first player, conductor or composer to vocalize a instrumental phrase or solo. Jazz singers of every generation are indebted to Louis Armstrong for giving voice to jazz.

Defining Scat

Scat singing is the vocalization of sounds and syllables that are musical but have no literal translation. Artists use different stylistic approaches similar to language dialects. To a certain extent, the choice of syllables is enigmatic, except to say that a sound, or its contrast with others, creates a syntax of its own. Scat is as old as jazz but has been regarded primarily as a bebop idiom. Bebop scat is often sung up-tempo; in fact, the whimsy of scat, its syllables and improvisatory style, may seem to clash with the poignancy of a slow tune. For Louis Armstrong, however, articulation and phrasing became an extension of his melodic embellishment on trumpet. It was natural for him to insert some scat obbligatos in the middle of a song, regardless of tempo.

Other instrumentalists and singers have adopted the characteristic sounds of bass, guitar, trombone and drums. In the late twenties, in bands such as Duke Ellington's, instrumentalists used tonguing techniques and mutes to imitate the human voice. Vocalists imitated the sounds of horns. It was almost as if the two "voices" became one, and at times it was difficult to be sure which was the horn and which the singer. This style, which might be called instru-vocal, was introduced by Ellington's singers, primarily Baby Cox, and by Leo Watson, an enormously talented yet little-known influence on scat vocalists for whom almost no recordings exist.

Ella Fitzgerald

Ella Fitzgerald grew up listening to Louis Armstrong and Connie Boswell, who rose to prominence in the thirties. Ella achieved her first professional success at the age of 17 when she won a talent show. While on tour with Chick Webb, she had her first hit, "A Tisket, A Tasket." When Webb died in 1939, Fitzgerald took over his band. She continued to utilize the Webb book, performing straight renditions of popular songs. In the early forties, she began to perform with a trio. The group, called Ella and her Bop Boys, consisted of legends-to-be Hank Jones, Roy Haynes and Ray Brown. During the forties, Ella became a virtuoso in the bop scat style.

In 1956, Fitzgerald began a series of songbooks of the popular song composers of the 20th century: Cole Porter, Irving Berlin, the Gershwins, Harold Arlen, Richard Rogers and Lorenz Hart, and Duke Ellington and Billy Strayhorn. Her voice was a light and limber instrument, enabling her to sing with facile articulation, speed and style. Her range and flexibility were extraordinary. As if in counterpoint to her light touch, she brought gravity to her interpretations. Without sacrificing the composer's meaning or melodic line, she embellished their songs with interesting improvisation and blues riffs. Ella's emphasis on musical content became even clearer when she moved out front as a soloist. During a career covering over five decades, Ella Fitzgerald established herself and remained a favorite of concert audiences around the world, performing at a high level well into her seventies. She appeared in several films and on television. Working with virtually all of her acclaimed contemporaries, she produced some of her finest collaborations with Ellington and Strayhorn, Count Basie, Louis Armstrong and arranger Nelson Riddle.

Ella Fitzgerald, a private person, has been adored but, regrettably, underappreciated. Perhaps her talent and facility, along with her joyful and uplifting persona, has led critics and listeners to mistake her simplicity and elegance for superficiality. Those who have criticized Ella Fitzgerald's range must be unfamiliar with the stretch between the sonorous chest voice heard in her 1957 recording of "Lush Life" and the soaring, perfectly tuned upper range in her Berlin concert performance of "How High the Moon." Although she may have lacked the sensuality of Billie Holiday or the knowingness of Sarah Vaughan, Ella brought stirring, authentic readings to America's treasure of popular song, maintaining the integrity of the melody and allowing the words to speak in the voices of the creators. When a song required sophistication, she soulfully captured its sadness and irony, as in her stunning version of "Miss Otis Regrets."

As a scat vocalist Ella was unrivaled. She took the bop idiom and adapted it to voice. Her improvisations were musically and verbally inventive, filled with the joy of her creativity. She and Louis Armstrong, whose recordings together are a singular delight, represent the essence and the pinnacle of scat singing.

Leo Watson

Leo Watson's influence is far greater than his fame. Watson (1898-1950) was Armstrong's contemporary. He led bands of his own, playing drums and the tiple, a Latin-American guitar. In the thirties he was a featured vocalist with big bands led by clarinetist Artie Shaw and drummer Gene Krupa. Watson had an impressive vocal range. Although capable of moving seamlessly in and out of falsetto, he frequently chose jarring shifts instead, for comic effect.

Where Armstrong might sing an entire chorus in an instrumental style, Watson was all over the place, using nonsense syllables, instrumental sounds, quotes from popular tunes, sound effects and humorous phrasing. At times he sang the melody, then improvised a counter-melody while one of the instrumentalists played the tune. Watson's voice became a line in the arrangement. In "Jada," one of his few available recordings, he inserted a trumpet-like riff as his own instrumental fill. His solo chorus in Jada nearly defies description. The opening phrase concludes with an unexpected obscenity, followed by another riff, and then a quote from "Jingle Bells." The second chorus features staccato rhythms. In tunes such as "Jada," Watson sings in the style of the swing era. But when he tackled the chord changes in "Night and Day," re-christened "Tight and Gay," he brought bop phrasing and embellishments to the song. His humorous renditions are imbued with the same sense of light-hearted absurdity later reintroduced by Bulee "Slim" Gaillard.

Instru-Vocal: The Old New Thing

The instru-vocal style of the twenties continued with the popular sound of the Mills Brothers and the Boswell Sisters in the thirties, and in the music of the Andrews sisters in the early forties. The Boswell Sisters, fronted by Connie Boswell, performed straight interpretations of popular songs. They utilized instrumental sounds in their presentations and pioneered the use of close harmonies, which also dominated the Andrews Sisters music during the following decade. While some have described the Boswells as reminiscent of barbershop singers of the turn of the century, their sound actually resembled horns playing in close harmony. In "If It Ain't Love," for example, Connie takes a solo chorus in which she unmistakably imitates a trumpet in sound and phrasing, and the sisters chime in with conventional big-band brass punctuation.

Although the Andrews Sisters were not truly scat singers, they became famous for their smooth harmonies and phenomenal blend. They extended the breadth of the singer's repertoire. Some of their more interesting numbers incorporated scat syllables and phrasing suggestive of what was later to become known as vocalese.

At the same time as the Boswell and Andrews families were performing with big bands, the bebop revolution was gathering steam. The bebop style, as practiced by Dizzy Gillespie, involved singing, although mostly as novelty. For many years Dizzy's band featured Joe Carroll, a singer who drew upon Leo Watson's style, particularly his humor. As instrumental boppers changed the music, a comparable bop vocal style evolved along with it. Its principal practitioner was Slim Gaillard. Noted for his flip, irreverent humor on and off the stage, Gaillard is remembered for combining his singing and guitar-playing with bassist Slam Stewart in the group Slim and Slam. He wrote his own songs, actually little more than routines, replete with satire, nonsense syllables and occasional twists on serious music styles. In Gaillard's vernacular, nearly everyone received the moniker of McVouty or o-Rooney, as in Charlie Parker-o-Rooney. His best known tunes are "Cement Mixer," "Puttee Puttee" and "Flat Foot Floogie with the Floy Floy."

Slim embodied the zoot-suited, beret-topped, goateed bebopper who played and talked jive. It is not known whether he coined such jive as "awreet" or simply popularized it. He was a hipster who defined hip with his act. He sang funny songs, novelties which were peppered with hipsterisms. He and Babs Gonzales furthered comedic scat singing in the bebop era. Gaillard,who died in 1991, can be seen in two films from the forties, *Star Spangled Rhythm* and *Hellzapoppin'*, in which Leo Watson also makes an appearance. Gaillard temporarily retired from the stage, eventually making a comeback by appearing as a singer in Roots—the Second Generation in 1982.

With the advent of 78 RPM singles, recordings lasting three minutes or less, individual songs became salable commodities. In general, scat vocals were not con-sidered marketable on their own. Performers such as Mel Torme and later Sarah Vaughan, alternated between recording lyrical songs and performing scat in live concerts and as a complement to instrumental compositions.

Vocalese

The vocalist's repertoire was expanded by the development of vocalese, the setting of lyrics to an instrumental jazz tune. One of the earliest examples of this style is Eddie Jefferson's lyricized rendition of Coleman Hawkins' ground-breaking 1939 performance of "Body and Soul." Jefferson's vocalization introduced a new dimension to jazz soloing, allowing the singer to take the improvised instrumental line and comment on it vocally. Jefferson wrote and performed lyrics to James Moody's solo of "I'm in the Mood for Love." Jefferson's interpretation, "Moody's Mood for Love" is the most famous example of early vocalese.

King Pleasure's recording of it landed high on the 1952 rhythm & blues charts. He followed this success with other legendary performances, such as his vocalese rendition of "Parker's Mood," which captured the heart-breaking sorrow of one of Charlie Parker's most deeply expressive blues performances.

Vocalese reached its greatest popularity in the fifties with the emergence of Lambert, Hendricks and Ross, a trio formed after each had achieved solo notoriety. Dave Lambert, originally a big band singer, was an early and fluent bebopper. He and singer Buddy Stewart moved away from the big band tradition to form a group fronted by drummer Gene Krupa, called the G-Notes, and had an early hit with the tune "What's This." The two singers then joined up with a group featuring trumpeter Red Rodney and such other bop stalwarts as Al Haig, Curly Russell and Stan Levey, making dynamic recordings of "Perdido" and "Charge Account" (based on the changes and Charlie Parker's introduction to Jerome Kern's "All The Things You Are"). Lambert's collaboration with Hendricks and Ross allowed him to showcase his under-stated approach, rhythmic precision, and wry scat lines—all integral to the success of the group.

Annie Ross, a British singer of ballads and bop, earned her reputation in the early fifties by writing and performing "Twisted," adding delightful vocalese to an upbeat blues tune and perky tenor sax solo by Wardell Gray. She began her career by recording with other instrumentalists, such as the late baritone saxophonist, Gerry Mulligan. A self-taught drummer and singer, Jon Hendricks was encouraged by Charlie Parker to turn professional rather than study law. He first reached success as a song writer for Louis Jordan, the great rhythm-and-blues innovator, who came to prominence in the forties. Hendricks ventured into vocalese by writing lyrics for Woody Herman's "Four Brothers" and "Cloudburst," an instrumental by Sam "The Man" Taylor based upon "I Got Rhythm." During the fifties, Hendricks also recorded with George Russell.

The Lambert, Hendricks and Ross trio were capable (with some overdubbing) of generating the sound and swing of a big band. They recorded two albums of material by Count Basie and retro-fitted classic solos by Lester Young, Harry Sweets Edison and other Basie luminaries. The group also recorded an album of Duke Ellington hits. Other performances included works by a variety of jazz composers of the day including Horace Silver, Randy Weston, Mongo Santamaria, Bobby Timmons and Cannonball Adderley. Annie Ross re-recorded "Twisted" for inclusion in the trio's repertoire. Their performances customarily included "Cloudburst," the Hendricks tour-de-force delivered in a flurry of words and notes—super-fast, clean and articulate. The group disbanded in 1962, after numerous awards and considerable record sales, when Annie Ross withdrew from the band. The talented Ceylonese singer, Yolande Bavan replaced Ross in the trio, but the new group lacked the flair that Ross brought to the mix. The group disbanded in 1964 and Dave Lambert died in 1966. Jon Hendricks continues to perform and write. Annie Ross has returned to singing and theatrical performance.

Betty Carter, still a vital force, began her career in the fifties. Like Ella Fitzgerald, she first caught attention by winning a talent show. She began as a singer of standards and blues, adding scat to her repertoire. Carter was recruited by Ray Charles for a duet album which remains one of Ray's most popular recordings. Today she remains one of the most fluid and masterful vocal improvisers. Like Art Blakey's Jazz Messengers, her band has been a training ground for young jazz musicians.

British vocalist Cleo Laine began her career in the fifties but did not become well known among American listeners until the late sixties. A versatile performer, she has recorded Fats Waller, Arnold Schoenberg and Stephen Sondheim and much else in between. Her husband, arranger and reed player John Dankworth, is her most frequent collaborator. She also has recorded with Annie Ross (Walton's *Facade*) Ray Charles (Gershwin's *Porgy and Bess*) James Galway and Dudley Moore. Laine has a big and powerful voice, full in the upper register, husky and sexy in the lower. Her trademark sound includes impeccable vocal doubling of Dankworth's smooth clarinet and saxophone lines.

Scat From the Sixties to the Nineties

The sixties were lean years for all but a few jazz performers. The experimental free-jazz movement with its small but dedicated following drove many mainstream artists out of jazz. Even well-known artists like Eddie Jefferson found themselves unable to sustain a career. One singer who came to the fore with his deep and resonant voice was Leon Thomas. Born Amosis

Leontopolis Thomas, his vocalese versions of jazz standards included unconventional vocal techniques. He routinely used what has been described as a "pygmy yodel," an oscillation between pitches that produces a droning effect. Many of his tunes included vocalization without words or syllables. His collaboration with saxophonist Pharaoh Sanders produced "The Creator Has a Master Plan," and other compositions strongly influenced by African musical traditions. Although long absent from the scene, Thomas recently has begun performing again and appears to be in fine voice.

As the sixties came to a close, jazz began to blur with the emerging rock and world music cultures. Many jazz groups began to incorporate electric pianos, electric guitars and synthesizers. The development of electronic instruments and the burgeoning sophistication of studio technique revolutionized all styles of music, including jazz. Jazz-rock or fusion bands began to push mainstream jazz to the side. Scat singing, while barely noticed in the free-jazz era, began to reappear in new contexts. Al Jarreau, a singer with great range and technique, became one of the first stars of the seventies who, backed by a group of outstanding fusion players, blended various styles of music, including scat. The Brazilian singer Flora Purim came to prominence as a member of Chick Corea's electric group, Return to Forever, and later recorded the beautiful and memorable "500 Hundred Miles High" and "You're Everything" with her husband Airto Moreira. Manhattan Transfer, which debuted in the early Seventies, is a mixed quartet whose repertoire has included vocalese and scat singing in a variety of arrangements. They group performs jazz-rock as well as mainstream pieces such as Eddie Jefferson's take on "Body & Soul." George Benson, having labored for years as an excellent mainstream electric guitarist, found his voice and became a singer who doubled his own vocal improvisations with guitar lines. Joni Mitchell and several other rock vocalists have tried their hand at Annie Ross's "Twisted." Finally, Eddie Jefferson re-emerged, performing and recording with alto saxist Richie Cole. Jefferson , who died in 1979, revived many of the great vocalese numbers and added some exciting new ones.

In the late seventies and early eighties, European singers such as Urszula Dudziak and Lauren Newton and Americans Bobby McFerrin and Jay Clayton began to expand the concept of scat singing, integrating folk elements, unconventional sounds and innovative vocal

14

techniques. Along with the author, Bob Stoloff, and vocalist/dancer, Jean Lee, these talented performers comprised Vocal Summit, an all-star a cappella team assembled by German music historian and producer, Joachim Berendt. This unique collaboration broke with convention to explore the outer limits of spontaneous vocal improvisation drawing upon the entire world of sound for source material.

Bobby McFerrin went on to become the best known contemporary instru-vocalist. Perhaps best known for the light-hearted, "Don't Worry, Be Happy," his musicianship is peerless, his ear precise and he is blessed with extraordinary range, sense of rhythm and vocal timbre. With one voice, McFerrin can achieve the complexity of an entire band, thumping drum beats on his chest while judiciously interspersing bass tones amid the melody line. He has established a standard for instru-vocal technique as it is now practiced.

Histories of this kind risk excluding some important artists and perhaps overstating the case for others. We cannot be certain whose work will influence the scat singers of the future. Time and taste will tell. Predictions are limited by our inability to see around corners or beyond the horizon. Nevertheless, anyone interested in scat or instru-vocal performance will have to cross paths with the artists portrayed here. It is our hope that students will ultimately discover their own style of creative expression.

Evan Sarzin

Chapter 1: Rhythmic Considerations

Syllable Articulation

The first question many novice level students ask is "Which syllables should I use to scat?" More seasoned improvisers complain that their syllables are too repetitive and sound "boring." Although I believe that scat syllables should be the unpredictable result of spontaneous musical expression rather than the primary focus of vocal improvisation, traditional scat singing does utilize particular syllable combinations that can be learned much as one learns a foreign language.

This chapter demonstrates traditional scat syllable articulation using non-pitched rhythmic phrases. The syllables presented are intended to be a point of departure and not a prescription for improvisation. Scat singers should first explore and experiment with spontaneous syllables.

Vowels and Accents

A phrase of any length will be effective if it has rhythmic equilibrium. This can be achieved by carefully integrating duple and triple rhythmic figures, ties, rests, articulation markings and accents. Syllables with carefully chosen vowel sequences, when added last, will enhance the phrase with coloration.

The most frequently used vowels in traditional scat singing are *ah, ee* and *oo.* Syllable combinations with 2 vowels (in the form of 8ths or 16ths, for example) must be used with reserve. *Du-be* and *da-be,* for example, may sound trite after several repetitions. Try combining these 2-syllable rhythms with triplets such as *du-ee-a* to alleviate this common problem.

Practice Rhythmic Etudes 1-4 to strengthen the articulation of duple and triple syllable combinations. Each exercise demonstrates various syllable combinations with particular attention to vowels. Stylistic accents have been added which may be interpreted with a jazz swing or Latin straight-8th feel.

Rhythm Etude 1

Swing feel

du dn du dn du dot   du dn du dn dah   du e a du dn du dot

du e a du dah———   du dn du e a du dot   du dn du e a dah

du dn du dn du e a dot   du e a du dah———   du e a du dn du e a du dn

du e a du e a du dn du dn   du dn du e a du dn du e a

du dn du dah———   ba du e a du dn du dn du e a

du dn du dn du e a du e a   du dn du e a du e a du dn

du dn du dah——— du dot ba du dot ba du dn du dn du dot ba

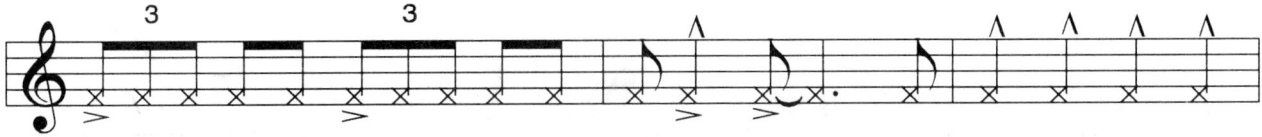

du e a du dn du e a du dn du dot dah——— bu dot dut dot dut

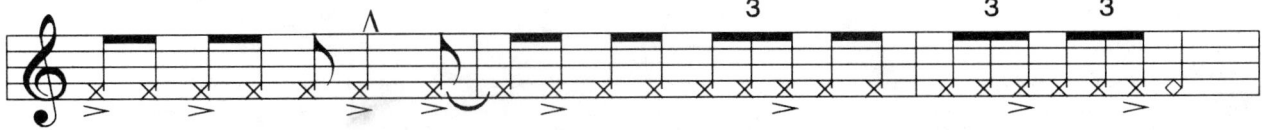

du dn du dn du dot da——— ba du dn du e a du dn du e a du e a dah

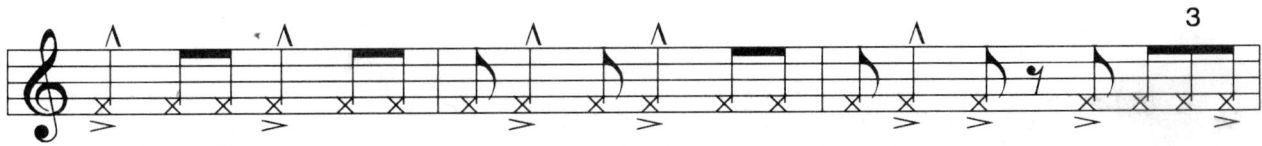

dot du dn dot du dn du dot bu dot du dn du dot dut ba du e a

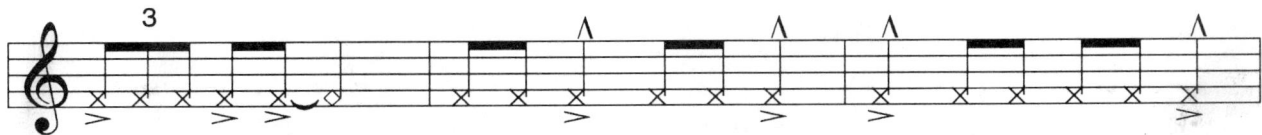

du e a du dah——— du dn dot du dn dot dut du dn du dn dot

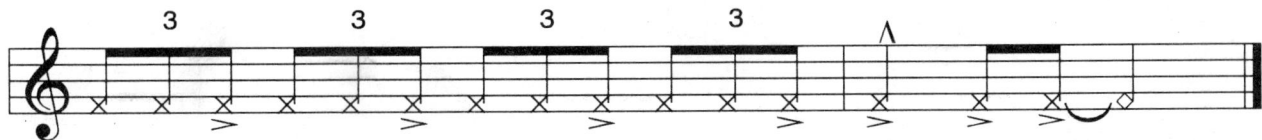

du e a du e a du e a du e a dot du dah———

Rhythm Etudes #1-4: First listen to CD tracks 1 and 4. I recorded the first 16 measures of each of these etudes to demonstrate correct articulation and vocal timbre. Once the notation is learned, keep practicing these exercises at different tempos by using a metronome. Start at 96 and increase your speed a little each day until you are able to articulate all 4 rhythm etudes at 160 with clarity and precision.

Rhythm Etude 2

Swing feel

du ba du dn dot   du ba du dn dot   du ba du dn du ba du dn

du ba du dn dot   du dn du ba dot   du dn du ba dot

du dn du ba du dn du ba   du dn du ba dot   du ba du dn du ba du dn

du ba du ba du dn du dn   du dn du ba du ba du dn

du ba du dn dot   du ba du ba du ba du dn   du dn du dn du dn du ba

dwe dot du dot dot du ya du dah___ du ba du dn du ba du dn
di da le di da le di da le di da le du dot du dot du ya___ ba de da ba de du dot
dweet du dn di da le dot di da le du dn dwe dn dot du ya du dn du ba du dn
du e a du e a dot du dot du dot ba dwe dn du dot
du dot dut dot ba di da le da ba dweet

Rhythm Etude 3

Swing feel

di da le da ba dwe ba da ba di da le dwe da di da le da ba di da le da ba

di da le di da le dot dwe dot ba da ba di da le di da le da ba dwe da

du dot dweet___ dot ba di da le du wah___ du ya du dn du dn di da le

du ba du ba di da le du dn du dwe ba di da le dot du ya du dah_____

dwe ba du dn dwe dot ba du dn du dn dwe dut da___ba de da ba de dweet du da___

dwe___ dut dot ba dwe ba di da le da ba di da le di da le dot du dn da ba du dn da ba   du dn du dah—   du ya du dn du dot

du ya du dn dot   du ya du dn du ya du dn   du ya du dot   bu

dot   du ya dot   du ya   du ya du dn dot   du ya   du dn du ya du dn du ya

du ya du dn dot   du dn du dn du ya du ya   du dn du ya du ya du dn

du ya dot   du ya dot   du ya du dn dot   bu dot   du ya du ya du ya

du dn du dn du dn du ya   du dn du ya du dn du ya   du ya du dot

Rhythm Etude 4

du ee a du dn di-da-le ba du dn du ee a du ee a di-da-le ba du dn

di-da-le ba du dn du ee a du dn di-da-le ba du ee a dot

du ee a di-da-le ba du ee a di-da-le ba du ee a du ee a di-da-le ba di-da-le ba

du dn di-da-le ba du ee a di-da-le ba di-da-le ba di-da-le ba dot

di-da-le ba du ee a du ee a di-da-le ba du ee a di-da-le ba di-da-le ba du ee a

di-da-le ba du ee a di-da-le ba du ee a di-da-le ba di-da-le ba di-da-le ba dot

du ee a du dn du dn di-da-le ba du dn di-da-le ba du ee a di-da-le ba

di-da-le ba di-da-le ba di-da-le ba di-da-le ba du ee a di-da-le ba dot

Recommended Scat Artists

Louis Armstrong

Leo Watson

The Boswell Sisters

The Rhythm Boys

The Mills Brothers

King Pleasure

Anita O'Day

Ella Fitzgerald

Lambert, Hendricks and Ross

Eddie Jefferson

Sarah Vaughan

Mel Tormé

Mark Murphy

Betty Carter

Janet Lawson

Sheila Jordan

Al Jarreau

Urszula Dudziak

Dee Dee Bridgewater

Jay Clayton

Jeanne Lee

Lauren Newton

Tania Maria

Bobbie McFerrin

Carmen McRae

Chet Baker

James Moody

Dizzy Gillespie

George Benson

Darmon Meader

Ray Anderson

Slam Stewart

Frank Rosolino

Conte Candoli

Clark Terry

Chapter 2: Melodic Considerations

Traditional Diatonic Patterns

After practicing syllable articulation, the three basic vowel sounds may be applied to scalar and intervallic patterns. A simple diatonic approach should be comfortable for most musicians, especially those familiar with traditional exercises. It is important to consider which vowels to use when a line is ascending or descending. In general, vowels sound better when *ee* is used for higher notes and *ah* or *oo* is assigned to the lower pitches. It is also important to add stylistic accents to certain syllables in the phrase. The choice of syllables to accent depends upon the type of melodic approaches used in the line. Note which syllables work best when the melodic contour changes direction and when the line moves by step or wider intervals.Some of these traditional patterns already have 8th, triplet and 16th feel variations added as an introduction to Latin, jazz and funk feels.

Begin with Scat Syllable Warm Up on page 26. It can be used as both a vocal warm up and as an articulation exercise using the three common vowels *ah, ee* and *oo* with consonants *b, d, l* and *n*. Note that syllables which end with l or n have no written vowel but are pronounced with a soft *i* sound (i.e. *dl* is pronounced *dil*). The syllable *dn* is somewhat challenging to articulate. It is produced by lifting the soft pallet and raising the tip of the tongue to the roof of the mouth so that the attack sounds like it originates from the nose. It is not pronounced as *din* which is how most beginners articulate this syllable. Practice with a straight-8th or swing-8th feel.

Scat Syllable Warm up

Swing or straight 8th

ba ba ba ba ba ba ba ba   ba ba ba ba ba ba ba ba   bah_____

da da da da da da da da   da da da da da da da da   dah_____

da ba da ba da ba da ba   da ba da ba da ba da ba   dah_____

di dl di dl di dl di dl   di dl di dl di dl di dl   dooh_____

bi dl bi dl bi dl bi dl   bi dl bi dl bi dl bi dl   booh_____

bi dl di dl bi dl di dl   bi dl di dl bi dl di dl   dooh_____

da dn da dn da dn da dn   da dn da dn da dn da dn   dah_____

ba dn ba dn ba dn ba dn   ba dn ba dn ba dn ba dn   bah_____

ba dn da dn ba dn da dn   ba dn da dn ba dn da dn   dah_____

du ee oo ee oo ee oo ee   du ee oo ee oo ee oo ee   dooh_____

This exercise can be sung with straight or swing 8ths. Beginners should start at 96 with a straight 8th feel. Work on the syllables that are the most challenging for you. Increase your speed gradually until you can articulate each line at a tempo of 144.

Traditional Diatonic Patterns

All patterns may be transposed to any desired key.

① du e du e du e du e du e du e da   dee a dee a dee a dee a

dee a dee a dee a da

1–3: Start at 144 and keep increasing your speed to the limit. Pay close attention to every accent marking.

② de a da ba de a da ba de a da ba de a da ba de a da ba de a da ba

de a da ba dah   du ee da ba du ee da ba du ee da ba du ee da ba

du ee da ba du ee da ba du ee da ba dah

③ da ba dee da ba dee da ba dee da ba dee da ba dee da ba dee da ba dee dah

dee ba da dee ba da dee ba da dee ba da dee ba da dee ba da dee ba da dah

4: This can be performed with or without chords. A good starting tempo is 160 which may be increased gradually to 208. The chords may be simplified by leaving out the 7ths and playing diatonic triads instead. Choose a key which will accomodate a comfortable range.

Jazz waltz feel
4
C Maj7
D min7
da ba da ba da ba da dee da da ba da ba da ba da dee da
E min7
F Maj7
da ba da ba da ba da dee da da ba da ba da ba da dee da
G7
A min7
da ba da ba da ba da dee da da ba da ba da ba da dee da
B m7(♭5)
C Maj7
da ba da ba da ba da dee da da ba da ba da ba dah
C Maj7
B m7(♭5)
dee ba da ba da ba dee da da dee ba da ba da ba dee da da
A min7
G7
dee ba da ba da ba dee da da dee ba da ba da ba dee da da
F Maj7
E min7
dee ba da ba da ba dee da da dee ba da ba da ba dee da da
D min7
G7
C Maj7
dee ba da ba da ba dee da da dee ba da ba da ba dah

Theme and Variations

Theme

bo ba da da bo ba da da bo ba da da bo ba da da bo ba da da bo ba da da

bo ba da da bo ba da da bo ba da da bo ba da da bo ba da da bo ba da da

bo ba da da bo ba da da bah

Variation 1

Latin feel

du ba du da du___ dwe du da du ba du da du___ dwe du da

du ba du da du___ dwe du da du ba du da du___ dwe du da

du ba du da du___ dwe du da du ba du da du___

dwe du da du ba du da du___ dwe du da dah

5 and 6: These are recorded on CD tracks 5 and 6 to demonstrate stylistic interpretation. Speed is not essential here so choose a moderate tempo. Pay close attention to the accents and the vowel placement.

Variation 2

Swing feel

dow   dwe   du   dwe   dow____   dwe   du   dwe   dow____   dwe   du   dwe   dow____

dwe   du   dwe   dow____   dwe   du   dwe   dow____   dwe   du   dwe   dow____

dwe   du   dwe   dow____   dwe   du   dwe   dow____   dwe   du   dwe   dow____

dwe   du   dwe   dow____   dwe   du   dwe   dow____   dwe   du   dwe   dow____

dwe   du   dwe   dow____   dwe   du   dwe   dah____

Variation 3

Funk feel

du da   ba du dn du da   ba du dn du da   ba du dn du da   ba du dn

du da   ba du dndu da   ba du dn du da   badudndu da   ba du dn du da   badudndu da   ba du dn

du da   ba du dn du da   ba du dn du da   badu dn du da   ba du dn dah

32

⑥ bwe bo bwe bobwebo bwe bo bwe bo bwe bobwe bo bwe bo bwe bo bwe bobwebo bwe bo

bwe bo bwe bo bwe bo bwe bo bwe bo bwe bo bwe bo bwe bo bah

⑦ du ee a du ee a du ee a du ee a du ee a du ee a du ee a dah

dee a ba dee a ba dee a ba dee a ba dee a ba dee a ba dee a ba dah

⑧ du ee da dn du ee da dn du ee da dn du ee da dn du ee da dn du ee da dn

du ee da dn dah dee a da dn dee a da dn dee a da dn dee a da dn

dee a da dn dee a da dn dee a da dn dah

7-11: Practice these patterns at tempos from 96 to 144. #9 thru 11 are better interpreted with straight 8ths.

12-A: Sing exactly as written from 72 to 126. 12-B: Try this one at tempos from 126 to 176.

13: This exercise is fun at faster tempos. Start at 96 and work your way up to 132. Note accents on the first beat of each measure.

da be da be da be da be da ba da ba da ba da ba   da be da be da be da be da ba da ba da ba da ba

da be da be da be da be da ba da ba da ba da ba   da be da be da be da be da ba da ba da ba da ba

da be da be da be da be da ba da ba da ba da ba   da be da be da be da be da ba da ba da ba da ba

da be da be da be da be da ba da ba da ba da ba   da be da be da be da be da ba da ba da

da be da be da be da be da ba da ba da ba da ba   da be da be da be da be da ba da ba da ba da ba

da be da be da be da be da ba da ba da ba da ba   da be da be da be da be da ba da ba da ba da ba

da be da be da be da be da ba da ba da ba da ba   da be da be da be da be da ba da ba da ba da ba

da be da be da be da be da ba da ba da ba da ba   da ba da be da be da be da ba da be dah

34

Swing feel

ba du dn du ya du dn dwe ba du dn dwe ba du dn dwe ba du dn du ya du dn

dwe ba du dn dwe ba du dn dwe ba du dn du ya du dn dwe ba du dn dwe ba du dn

dwe ba du dn du ya du dn dwe ba du dn dwe ba du dn dah

ba da da de da da da bo ba da da de da da da bo ba da da de da da da

bo ba da da de da da da bo ba da da de da da da bo ba da da de da da da

bo ba da da de da da da bo ba da da de da da da ba ba da de da da da

bo ba da da de da da da bo ba da da de da da da bo ba da da de da da da

bo ba da da de da da da bo ba da da de da da da bo ba da da de da da da

bo ba da da de da da da bah

14: du ee u dn du ba du ee u dn du ba du ee u dn du ba du ee u dn du ba

du ee u dn du ba du ee u dn du ba du ee u dn du ba dah

du ee u dn du ba du ee u dn du ba du ee u dn du ba du ee u dn du ba

du ee u dn du ba du ee u dn du ba du ee u dn du ba dah

15: dee a da dee a da dee a da dee a da dee a da dee a da dee a da dee

du ee a dah ee a du ee a dah ee a du ee a dah ee a du ee a dah

14: This is a jazz waltz feel so start around 132 with variations up to 200. Note the pick-up accent on the end of every third beat.

15: Practice with a 2-feel (dotted quarter=116 to 160).

II–V Modal Jazz Patterns

The following melodic exercises include 2–measure phrases which ascend and descend using scalar and intervallic approaches. Harmonically, each pattern conforms to the Dorian–Mixolydian, or II–V modal relationship. This simply means that the representative major scale for each key, usually beginning and ending with *do* can be sung starting on the second degree *re* and fifth degree *sol*. The resulting scales are called modes (see page 52) and in this case we are using Dorian mode *re–mi–fa–sol–la–ti–do–re* and Mixolydian mode *sol–la–ti–do–re–mi–fa–sol* as a harmonic guide on which the melodic pattern is built. Dorian mode is represented by minor 7th chords while Mixolydian uses the dominant 7th. Note that both scales are different starting positions for their related tonic scale or *do–re–me–fa–sol–la–ti–do*. The scale for the key of C, for example, is C–D–E–F–G–A–B–C. To sing Dorian mode we simply start on the second degree of the C scale which is the note D and continue until we reach the next D an octave higher (D–E–F–G–A–B–C–D). Mixolydian begins with the 5th scale degree which would be G–A–B–C–D–E–F–G. For additional modes see page 52 (Chapter 3: Melodic Considerations).

Each example should be performed in all keys using what is commonly called the Cycle of 5ths: a sequence of all 12 chromatic pitches that keep modulating up a fourth or down a fifth until every key is reached. This may be accomplished using one note (C–F–Bb–Eb, etc.), one type of chord (Cmaj7–Fmaj7–Bbmaj7–Ebmaj7, etc.) or a patterned chord progres–sion such as Dmin7–G7 to Cmin7–F7 to Bbmin7–Eb7, etc. This last example would be described as a II–V chord pattern modulating via cycle 5.

One-Measure II-V Patterns

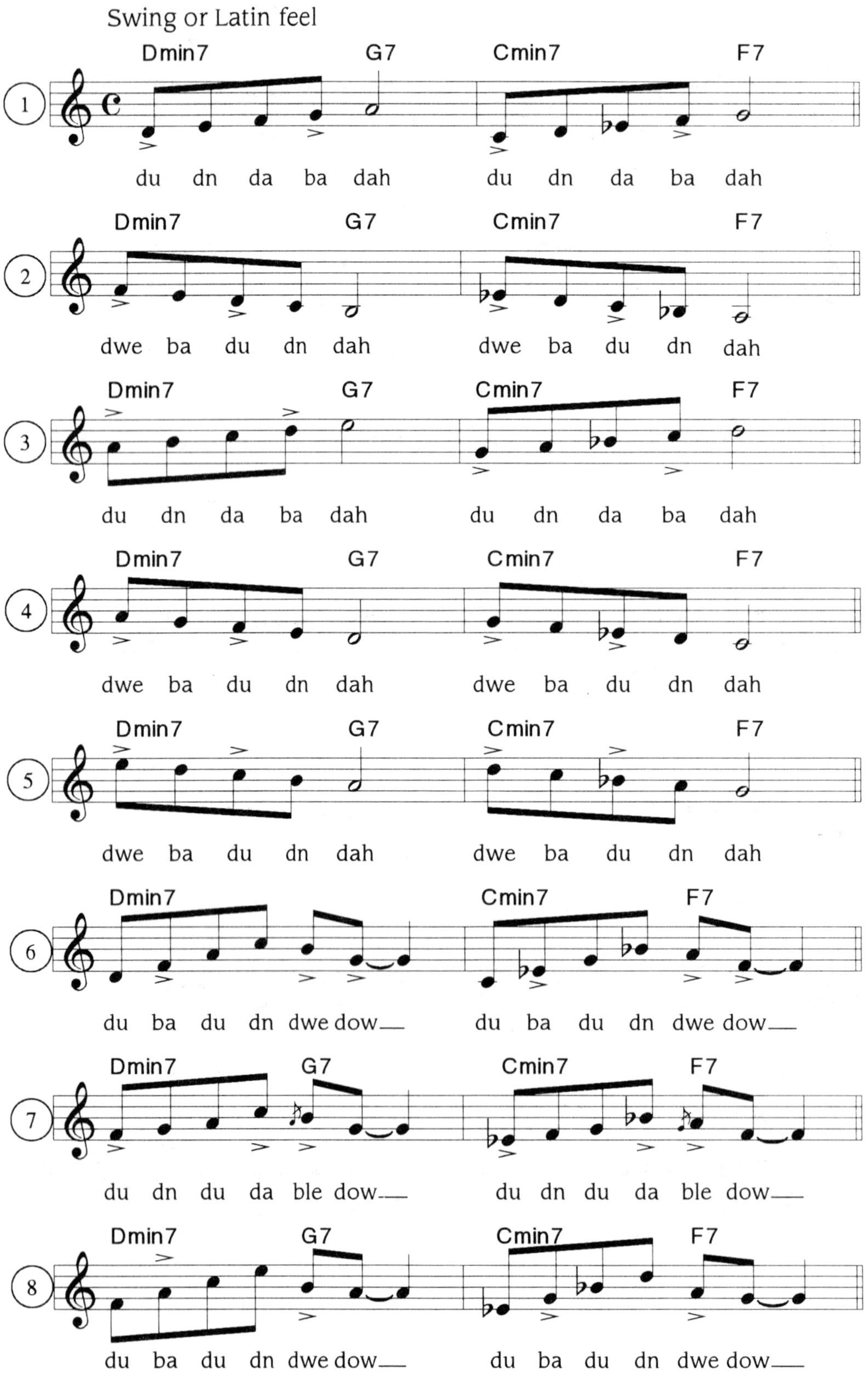

9
Dmin7 3 G7 Cmin7 3 F7
dwe da ba du dwe dow dwe da ba du dwe dow
10
Dmin7 G7 Cmin7 F7
dwe ba du dn du we dwe ba du dn du wee
11
Dmin7 G7 Cmin7 F7
dwe dn du ba du wee dwe dn du ba du wee
12
Dmin7 G7 Cmin7 F7
dwe ba du dn du wah dwe ba du dn du wah
13
Dmin7 G7 Cmin7 F7
dwe ba du dn du wee dwe ba du dn du wee
14
Dmin7 G7 Cmin7 F7
du ba du dn dah du ba du dn dah
15
Dmin7 G7 Cmin7 F7
de ba du dn dwe dow de ba du dn dwe dow
16
Dmin7 G7 Cmin7 F7
dwe dn du dn du yah dwe dn du dn du yah

Two-Measure II-V Patterns

Swing or Latin feel

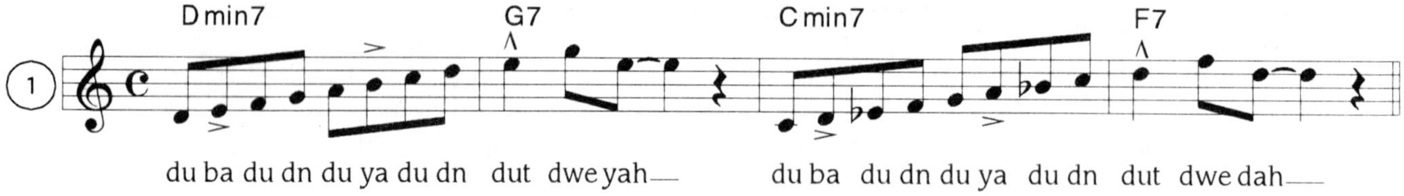

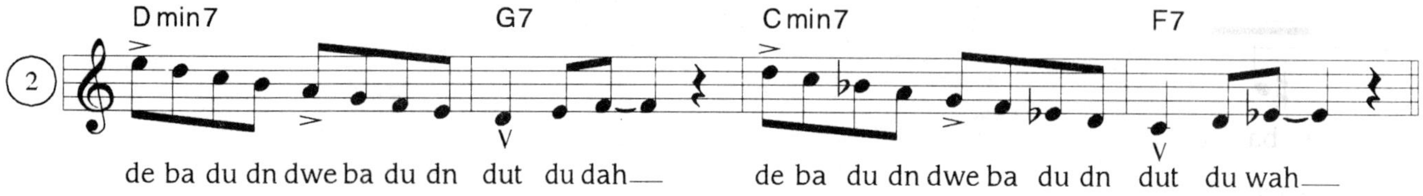

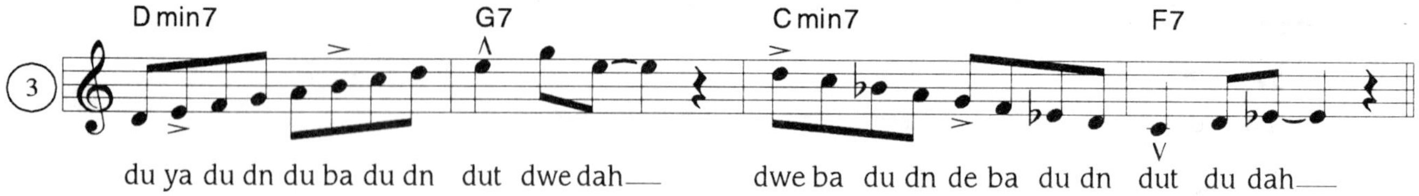

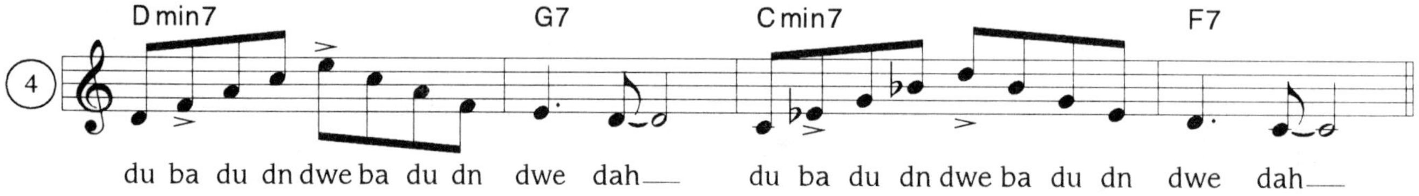

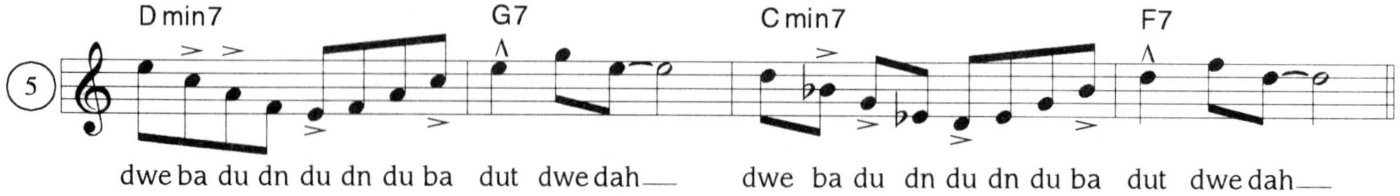

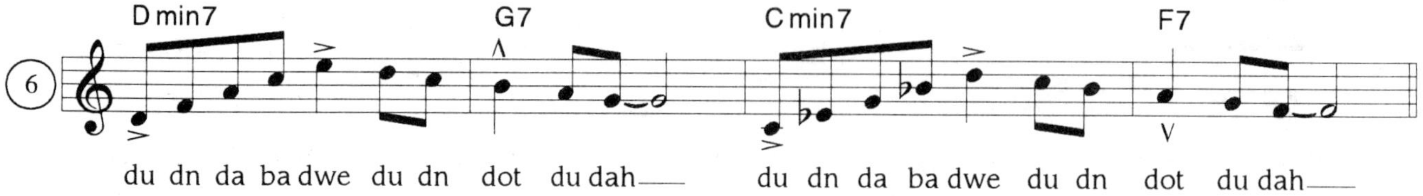

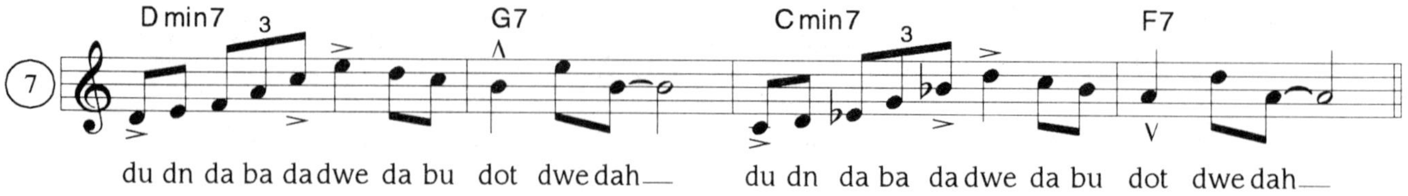

8
D min7
G7
dwe bu da ba da dwe ba du dn dut dwe yah
C min7
F7
dwe bu da ba da dwe ba du dn dut dwe yah
9
D min7
G7
dwe ba du dn du ya da ba dwe da ba du dwe dow
C min7
F7
dwe ba du dn du ya da ba dwe da ba du dwe dow
10
D min7
G7
dwe da ba da du dn dwe ba du be a dn dwe dow
C min7
F7
dwe da ba da du dn dwe ba du be a dn dwe dow
11
D min7
G7
C min7
dwe ba du dn du ya da ba dut dwe dow dwe da bu da dwe dn du ba
F7
B♭min7
E♭7
dwe ba du dn dwe dah dwe ba du dn du ya da ba dut dwe yah
A♭min7
D♭7
dwe da bu da dwe dn du ba dwe ba du dn dwe dah

Melodic Embellishment

Embellishing a musical phrase is a common practice in both classical music and jazz. In classical music, specific embellishments such as the mordant, turn, appoggiatura, grace note, trill and glissando are used to enhance a melodic sequence and make it more dramatic. Classical musicians may not have heard musical terms like "plop," "flip," "shake," "spill," "smear," or "doit" (pronounced *doyt*) which are used in standard big band arrangements such as those performed by the great big bands of Count Basie or Duke Ellington. Although not used frequently by scat singers, big-band embellishments can be very effective.

One of the more common vocal embellishments is the triplet figure *du-ee-a* (or *di-da-le*) which is often used in descending scalar patterns. In the following exercises triplet figures have been inserted on beats one or two (sometimes both) of the II minor pattern which then resolves to its related V7. Practice these line embellishment exercises in all keys via cycle 5.

Melodic Embellishment

1-Measure Phrases Using II-V

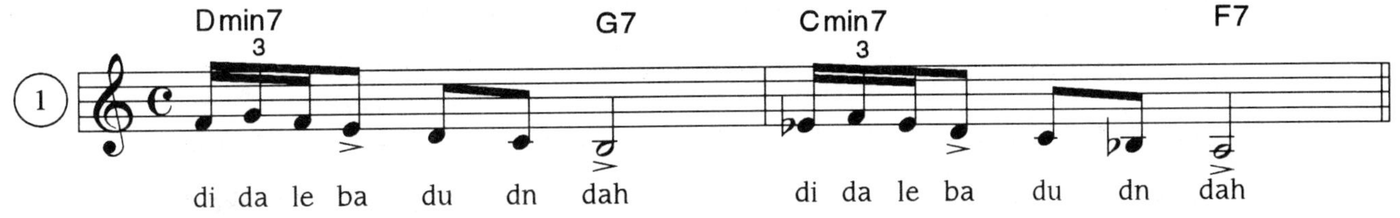

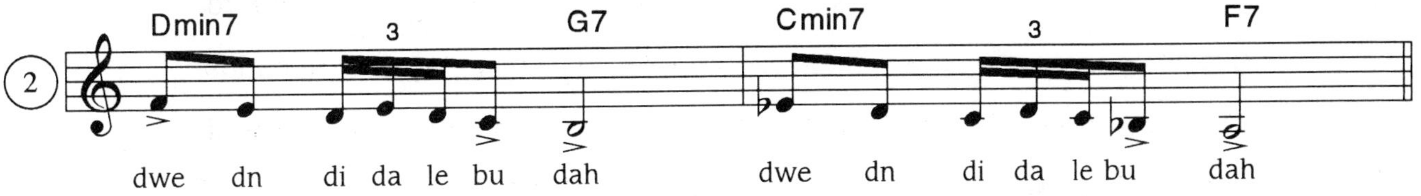

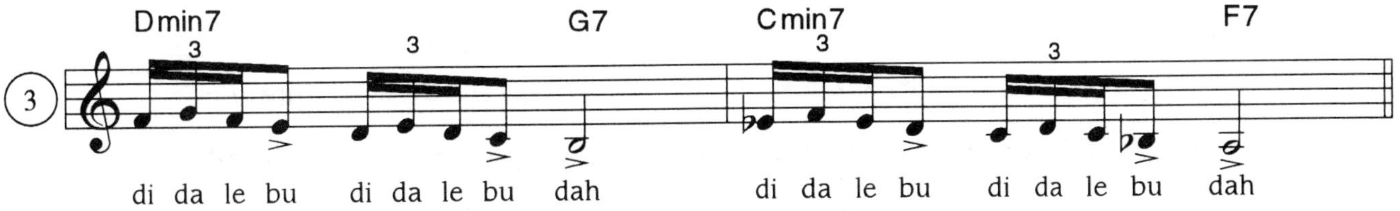

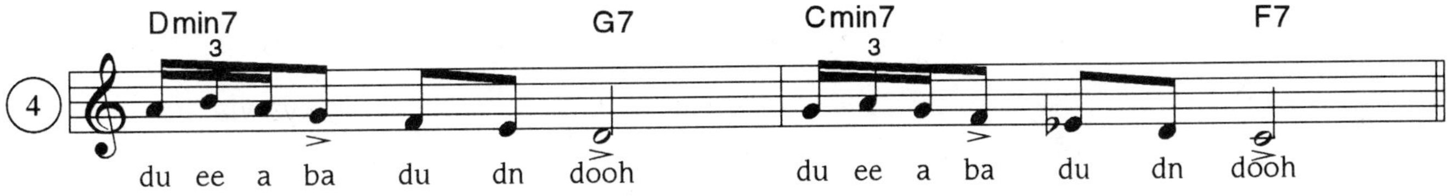

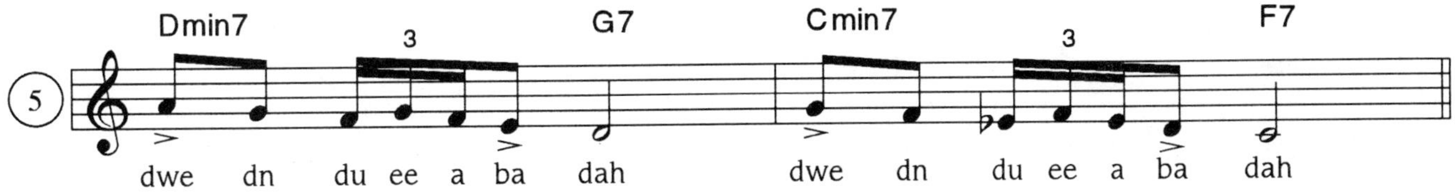

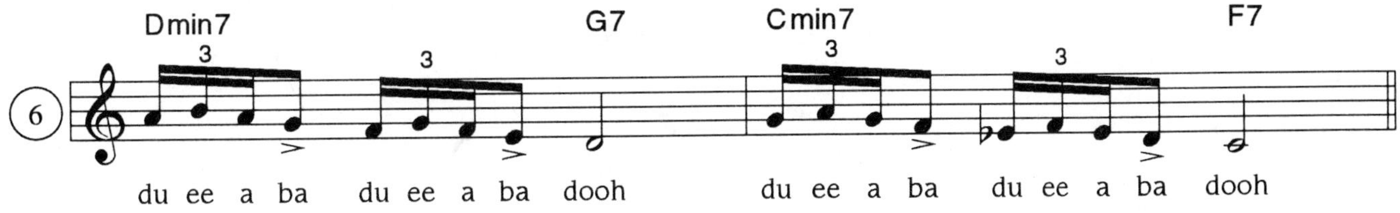

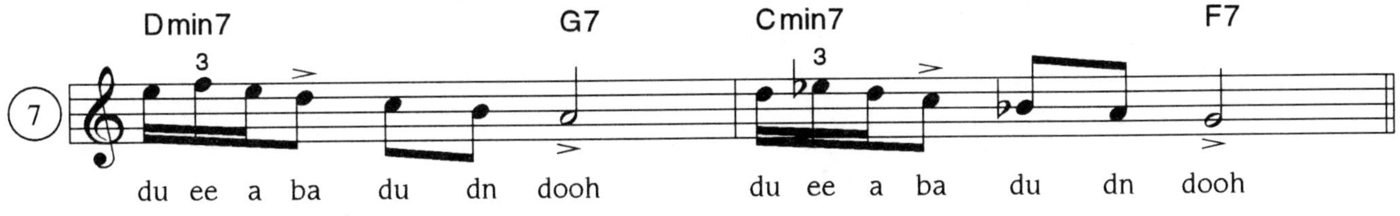

8. dwe dn du ee a ba dooh   dwe dn du ee a ba dooh

9. du ee a ba du ee a ba dooh   du ee a ba du ee a ba dooh

10. di da le ba du dn du dwe____   di da le ba du dn du dwe____

11. dwe dn di da le ba du dwe____   dwe dn di da le ba du dwe____

12. di da le ba di da le ba du dwe____   di da le ba di da le ba du dwe____

13. di da le ba du dn dwe dah____   di da le ba du dn dwe dah____

14. du dn du ee a ba dwe dah____   du dn du ee a ba dwe dah____

15
Dmin7 G7 Cmin7 F7
du ee a ba du ee a ba du dwe du ee a ba du ee a ba du dwe
16
Dmin7 G7 Cmin7 F7
di da le ba dwe dn du dah di da le ba dwe dn du dah
17
Dmin7 G7 Cmin7 F7
dwe dn du ee a ba dwe dah dwe dn du ee a ba dwe dah
18
Dmin7 G7 Cmin7 F7
du ee a ba du ee a ba dwe dah du ee a ba du ee a ba dwe dah
19
Dmin7 G7 Cmin7 F7
di da le ba du dn dwe dah di da le ba du dn dwe dah
20
Dmin7 G7 Cmin7 F7
du ee a ba du dn dwe dow du ee a ba du dn dwe dow
21
Dmin7 G7 Cmin7 F7
du ee a ba du ee a ba dwe dow du ee a ba du ee a ba dwe dow

II-V Pattern Etude

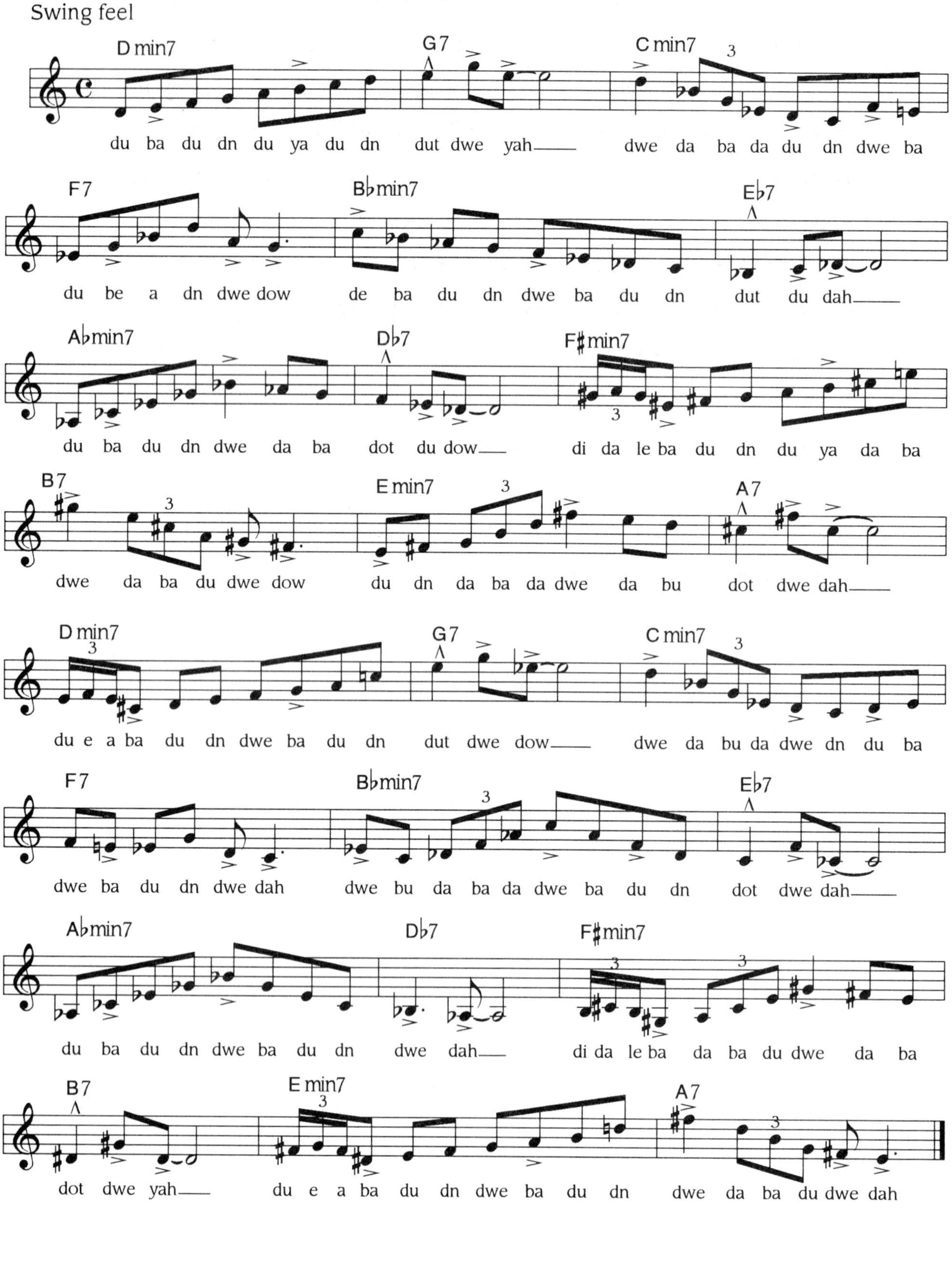

Line Contour

Line contour, or melodic shape, is an important consideration when improvising. A melody needs to move to the rhythmic pulse of the music and there are only two directions it can go: up or down. The way in which a melody moves from note to note is called "melodic approach." There are three basic melodic approaches: step, leap and half step. Approach by step means using a scale to move up or down, a leap is any interval of a 3rd or more and half steps resolve by moving chromatically in either direction. Intervallic movement is best practiced using arpeggios which outline each chord while scalar patterns require the correct chord scale for each type of chord. The integration of these two approaches with added chromaticism will yield excellent line contour.

The following exercises highlight some common scale and arpeggio approaches applied to the extended II–V chord pattern, a sequence of harmonically unrelated II–V's.

Extended II-V Arpeggio Approach

Swing feel

du ba du dn du dot du ba du dn du dot du ba du dn du du dah——

du ba du dn du dot du ba du dn du dot du ba du dn du du dah——

du ba du dn du dot du ba du dn du dot du ba du dn du du dah——

du ba du dn du dot du ba du dn du dot du ba du dn du du dah——

du ba du dn du dot du ba du dn du dot du ba du dn du du dah——

du ba du dn du dot du ba du dn du dot du ba du dn du du dah——

A♭min7 D♭7 B♭min7 E♭7 A♭min7 D♭7 G♭Maj7
du ba du dn du dot du ba du dn du dot du ba du dn du du dah
C♯min7 F♯7 D♯min7 G♯7 C♯min7 F♯7 BMaj7
du ba du dn du dot du ba du dn du dot du ba du dn du du dah
F♯min7 B7 G♯min7 C♯7 F♯min7 B7 EMaj7
du ba du dn du dot du ba du dn du dot du ba du dn du du dah
Bmin7 E7 C♯min7 F♯7 Bmin7 E7 AMaj7
du ba du dn du dot du ba du dn du dot du ba du dn du du dah
Emin7 A7 F♯min7 B7 Emin7 A7 DMaj7
du ba du dn du dot du ba du dn du dot du ba du dn du du dah
Amin7 D7 Bmin7 E7 Amin7 D7 GMaj7
du ba du dn du dot du ba du dn du dot du ba du dn du du dah

Extended II-V Altered Scale Approach

Abmin7 Db7 Bb-7b5 Eb7b9 Abmin7 Db7#9
3
du ba du dn dwe ba du dn du dn du ba du e a du dn du dn du ba de ya du dn
GbMaj7 C#min7 F#7 Eb-7b5 Ab7b9
3
dah du ba du dn dwe ba du dn du dn du ba du e a du dn
C#min7 F#7#9 BMaj7 F#min7 B7
du dn du ba de ya du dn dah du ba du dn dwe ba du dn
G#-7b5 C#7b9 F#min7 B7#9 EMaj7
3
du dn du ba du e a du dn du dn du ba de ya du dn dah
Bmin7 E7 C#-7b5 F#7b9 Bmin7 E7#9
3
du ba du dn dwe ba du dn du dn du ba du e a du dn du dn du ba de ya du dn
AMaj7 Emin7 A7 F#-7b5 B7b9
3
dah du ba du dn dwe ba du dn du dn du ba du e a du dn
Emin7 A7#9 DMaj7 Amin7 D7
du dn du ba de ya du dn dah du ba du dn dwe ba du dn
B-7b5 E7b9 Amin7 D7#9 GMaj7
3
du dn du ba du e a du dn du dn du ba de ya du dn dah

Chapter 3: Melodic Considerations

Modes

Modes are simply scales that use the same tones as the major scale but start on all scale steps in addition to the root, or *do*. The major scale itself is a modal scale called Ionian. Using the traditional Italian solfeggio syllables the notes would be called *do–re–mi–fa–sol–la–ti–do*. Each mode begins on a scale step and ends on the same tone an octave above. If we sing a scale starting on *re* and ascending one octave to the next *re*, the resulting scale is called the Dorian mode. Starting with the root, the modes are known as Ionian, Dorian, Phrygian, Lydian, Mixolydian, Aeolian and Locrian. This relationship of modal scales exists in all 12 keys. In the key of Ab, for example, the Dorian scale would begin on the note Bb and continue for one octave using the diatonic notes of the Ab major scale. Modes, then, may be considered scales which start on various degrees (or steps) of any major scale using only pitches that are diatonic to that major scale.

Modes may also be considered altered major scales, each with its own variation of raised or lowered steps which make it characteristically different from the others. C lydian, for example, can be considered a C major scale with alterations. To make any major scale a Lydian mode we simply raise the 4th scale step by one half. In this example the resulting scale notes are C–D–E–F#–G–A–B–C. We say that the characteristic note in Lydian mode that changes it from a major scale is a raised 4th degree. Note that C Lydian can also be thought of as G major but starting from its 4th degree, C. Each mode has different characteristic notes which alter them from their related major scales:

•Ionian: same as major scale

•Dorian: flat 3 and flat 7

•Phrygian: flat 2, flat 3, flat 6 and flat 7

•Lydian: sharp 4

•Mixolydian: flat 7

•Aeolian: flat 3, flat 6 and flat 7 (natural minor)

•Locrian: flat 2, flat 3, flat 5, flat 6 and flat 7

Jazz musicians often use modal scales as a melodic alternative to more traditional ways of improvising. Instead of using a separate scale for each chord it is possible to improvise over several related chords with just one mode. For example consider the chord progression Cmaj7–Amin7–Dmin7 to G7 (Imaj7–VImin7–IImin7–V7 in the key of C). An Ionian scale beginning on C ("C Ionian") will work perfectly for the entire duration of this chord pattern.

Modal Scales

Modes Related to One Scale

C Ionian   D Dorian

E Phrygian   F Lydian

G Mixolydian   A Aeolian

B Locrian

Modes as Altered Major Scales

C major

D Dorian   E Phrygian

F Lydian   G Mixolydian

A Aeolian   B Locrian

Chord Scales

The most important melodic consideration is, of course, singing the correct notes on each chord. There are five basic catagories of chords: major, minor, dominant, diminished and half diminished. Chord symbols represent different tonalities and signify the use of one or more characteristic scales. (For a complete scale syllabus consult any of Jamey Aebersold's publications which contain scalar variations as applied to jazz, Latin and pop music)

The following is an effective approach to improvising on a chord scale:

•**Step 1** Play the chord and then sing the appropriate scale from root position, ascending and descending at least one octave while the chord is still sounding.

•**Step 2** While sounding the chord, sing an arpeggio including the 3rd, 5th and 7th steps (pentatonic would include 1, 3, 5 and 6) ascending and descending at least one octave.

•**Step 3** Keep sounding the chord and sing some traditional patterns that match the tonality of the chord, beginning with the root.

•**Step 4** Sound the chord again and this time, in a rubato style, try to improvise your own patterns in the form of short phrases. Take as much time as necessary until you feel comfortable with the tonality of the chord and satisfied with your phrases.

Major 6th and 7th Chords

Major and pentatonic scales are used to improvise on major triads, maj6th and maj7th chords. Starting in root position, C maj6 or C maj7 would use either a pentatonic or major scale starting from C. Likewise, a Bb maj6 or Bbmaj7 would start on the note Bb, and so on for all major keys. The notes in a pentatonic scale are major scale steps 1, 2, 3, 5 and 6. Following the procedure above, try the following exercises which are derived from the Maj6 and Maj7 chord structure.

Basic Chord Scales

CMaj7(6) *Ionian*

du dn du ba du dn du ee   de a du dn de a da   du du du dwe du du   dah

Pentatonic

du dn du ba du dn du ba   du dn du ba du dn du ba   de ba du dn de ba du dn   de ba du dn de ba du dn

du   da   du   dwe   da   du   dah   du   du   dwe   da

dwe a du dn   du   ba dwe ba du dn   du ba du dn du dwe   ba   de   a   da   bu

du   we   dah

Dmin7 *Dorian*

du dn du ba du dn du ee   de a du dn de a da   du du du dwe du du   dah

Improvisation

da du da   ba   dwe du   da bu da dn   dwe da ba du dwe bu   da   du dn du we a ba

dwe   du   dah

Mixolydian

G7

du dn du ba du dn du ee   de a du dn de a da   du du du dwe du du dah

Improvisation

da ba du dwe___ ba du dn de a du dn da   ba de a du dn da bu dwe dn da ba

de a de a de a de a dah

Bm7♭5 *Locrian*

du dn du ba du dn du ee   de a du dn de a da   du du du dwe du du dah

Improvisation

du da ba dwe dn da ba dwe bu da de a da du we e a du dn

du dwe ba du ya du dn du e a du ba dwe dn du ya dah

C°7 *Diminished*

du dn du ba du dn du ba de a da ba de a da ba da du du dwe du du dah

Improvisation

dwe da ba du ee a dn dwe da ba du ee a dn dwe da ba de a de a

dwe ba du dn dwe ba du dn dwe de a da dah

C M+4 *Lydian*   Improvisation

du dn da ba dwe ba du dn de a da ba de a da da du dn dwe da

de a de a de a da ba du dwe da ba du dwe a du dn de a da de a da dah

Minor 7th Chords

In a minor 7th chord the major scale is altered by lowering the 3rd and 7th steps. The resulting scale with flat 3 and flat 7 is called Dorian mode. This scale, along with minor pentatonic, is most often used on minor 7th chords. The Minor pentatonic scale stems from its relative major.

C minor7, for example, has the same notes as Eb major pentatonic but begins on C (C, Eb, F, G, Bb). Although there are several other scale possibilities, these two are the strongest.

Try the following exercises which are derived from the minor 7th chord structure.

Additional Minor Scales

Ascending melodic minor

Improvisation

Minor pentatonic

Improvisation

Harmonic minor

Improvisation

du ba dwe dn de a da ba   dwe du dn du ba du dn   dwe ba dwe dn de a du dn   dah

Aeolian (natural minor)

Cmin (add b6)

du ba du dn du dn du ba   de a da ba du dn da

Improvisation

du dn du ee du dn da   de a da da ba de de a da du ba   du ee a du dn du ee a du dn

du ee a du dn dah

Cmin (b6 and b9)   *Phrygian*

du dn da ba du ba du dn   de a da ba du dn da

Improvisation

du e du dn du   da ba da de ba du dn du e da

du dn de ba da da ba da de ba da   du e a du dn du dn du ba dah

Altered Dominant 7th Chords

In a dominant 7th chord the major scale is altered by lowering the 7th degree by a half step. The chord written as G7, for example, implies the G major scale but uses F natural instead of F sharp. Another way to describe a dominant 7th chord is to label it a V7 of I in any key. Viewed in this way, a G7 chord is a V7, or "dominant 7th," of its related *I* which is, in this case, the key of C. The scale begins on G but has the key signature of C which has no accidentals. This scale is called Mixolydian mode and is one of the modal scales discussed on page 52.

Additional tensions give the dominant 7th chord the most scalar possibilities. A tension is a 9th, 11th or 13th scale degree positioned above the octave. A 9th, for example, is a major 2nd above the root of the chord but written an octave above. The 11th is an interval of one octave plus a perfect 4th above the root and the 13th is an octave plus a 6th above the root. Tensions may be raised or lowered by a half step to further enrich the harmony of the chordal tones. Each combination of natural, raised or lowered tensions implies a different chord scale although basic Mixolydian mode will work for all. Dominant 7th chords offer more options for altered scales because all tensions are available or sound reasonably good to the ear. With other chord types only some tensions are considered good choices.

Each of the following exercises uses a different altered dominant scale depending the available tensions. Remember to keep sounding the chord while singing each pattern.

Altered Dominant Scales

Blues scale   Improvisation

da ba da bu da bu dwe bu da de a du dah   du du dn dwe du dn

du e a du e a de a da de a da dwe du dn dwe ba du dah___

Bebop scale

da ba du dn du dn dwe ba de a du dn dwe ba du dn dow

Improvisation

dwe ba du dn de ba du e a de ba du dn du e a dwe dn du ba dwe dn dah

C 7+4   *Lydian dominant*   Improvisation

Tension #11

da ba du dn dwe ba du dn de a da bu dwe dn da   de ba

du dn dwe dn du ba du dn dwe de a ba dwe dn dwe dn

du dn da ba de a da dwe ba du dot

Jewish (harmonic minor)

C7♭9 — Tension ♭9

da ba du dn dwe ba du dn de a da bu dwe dn da

Improvisation

du ba du dn dwe du dn dwe ba du dn du du dn du e a de a da dwe du dn

du e a du dn du e a du dn du e a de a da dah

Symmetrical diminished

Tension #11
Tension ♭9   C7#9   Tension #9

du dn da ba dwe dn da ba de a du dn dwe a du dn

Improvisation

dah   du ba du dn dwe ba du dn du ba du dn dwe ba dwe dn

du e a du e a du ba du dn de a da de a da dwe ba du dn dah

Hindu — C7♭13

Tension ♭13

du ba du dn dwe ba du dn dwe ba du dn dwe ba da da bu da dwe ba

du dn du dn dwe da bu da dwe dn dwe dn de a da dwe dn du e a dwe a du dah

Diminished whole tone — C7♯9

Tension ♯11 / Tension ♭9 / Tension ♯9

du ba du dn du ba du dn dwe dn du ba dwe dn da

Improvisation

du ba du dn dwe a da dwe a da de a ba du e a du ba du dn

dwe dn dwe dn du e a dwe dn dah

Whole tone — C7+

Improvisation

da ba du dn da ba du dn de a da ba de a da du ba dwe da ba

de a da de a da dwe dn du dn dwe de a da du ee de a da bu dwe

Hom-in-a Hom-in-a Hom-in-a Hom-in-a.
Ralph Kramden

Skid-a-lee da-ba doo.
Popeye

Hi-dee-Hi-dee Ho!
Cab Calloway

Ooh bop shu-bam a klook-a mop.
Dizzy Gillespie

Inca-dinca-doo.
Jimmy Durante

Shoo-bee-doo-bee-doo.
Frank Sinatra

Ba-ba-ba-boo.
Bing Crosby

Dom Dom dom-a-doo-dom, a doo-bee doo.
Everly Brothers

Boop boop-be-doop!
Betty Boop

Idala-idala-idala-dala-idala—That's all, folks!
Porky Pig

Ya-ba-da-ba-doo!
Frederick Flintstone

Dominant 7th Phrases With Walking Bass Line

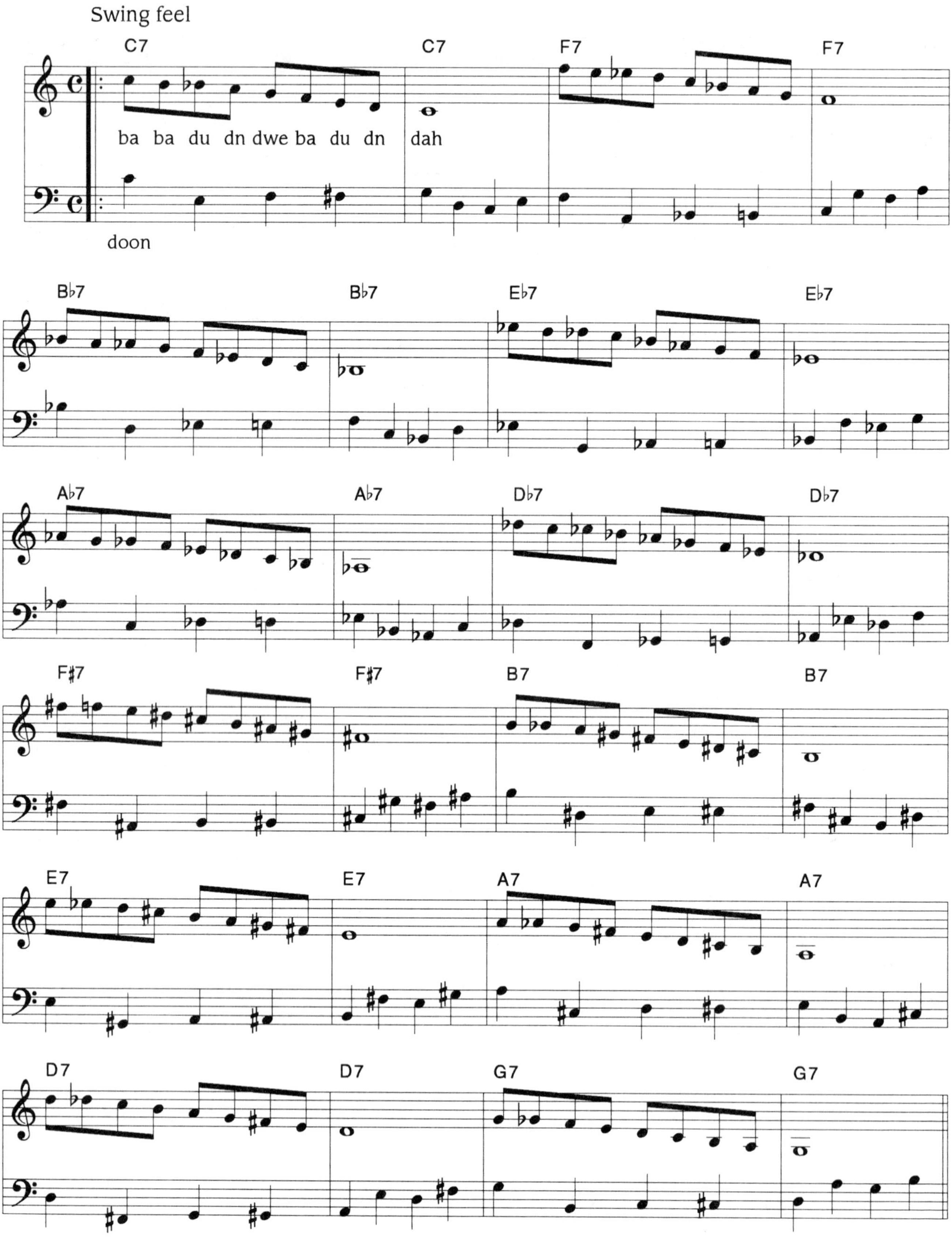

dwe dn du ba du ee du dn du bah___

Dominant 7th With Sharp 11

Swing feel

da da ba du ba dee dn   di da le du dn de da   da da ba du ba dee dn   di da le du dn de da

da da ba du ba deedn   di da le du dn de da   da da ba du ba dee dn   di da le du dn de da

da da ba du ba deedn   di da le du dn de da   da da ba du ba dee dn   di da le du dn de da

da da ba du ba dee dn   di da le du dn de da   da da ba du ba dee dn   di da le du dn de da

da da ba du ba dee dn   di da le du dn de da   da da ba du ba dee dn   di da le du dn de da

da da ba du ba deedn   di da le du dn de da   da da ba du ba deedn   di da le du dn de da

Dominant 7th Turnaround

E7 C♯7 F♯7 B7 EMaj7
du ba du dn dwe ba du dn du dn dwe ba du ba du dn dah
A7 F♯7 B7 E7 AMaj7
du ba du dn dwe ba du dn du dn dwe ba du ba du dn dah
D7 B7 E7 A7 DMaj7
du ba du dn dwe ba du dn du dn dwe ba du ba du dn dah
G7 E7 A7 D7 GMaj7
du ba du dn dwe ba du dn du dn dwe ba du ba du dn dah
C7 A7 D7 G7 CMaj7
du ba du dn dwe ba du dn du dn dwe ba du ba du dn dah
F7 D7 G7 C7 FMaj7
du ba du dn du ba du dn du ba du dn du ba du dn dah
B♭7 G7 C7 F7 B♭Maj7
du ba du dn du ba du dn du ba du dn du ba du dn dah
E♭7 C7 F7 B♭7 E♭Maj7
du ba du dn du ba du dn du ba du dn du ba du dn dah

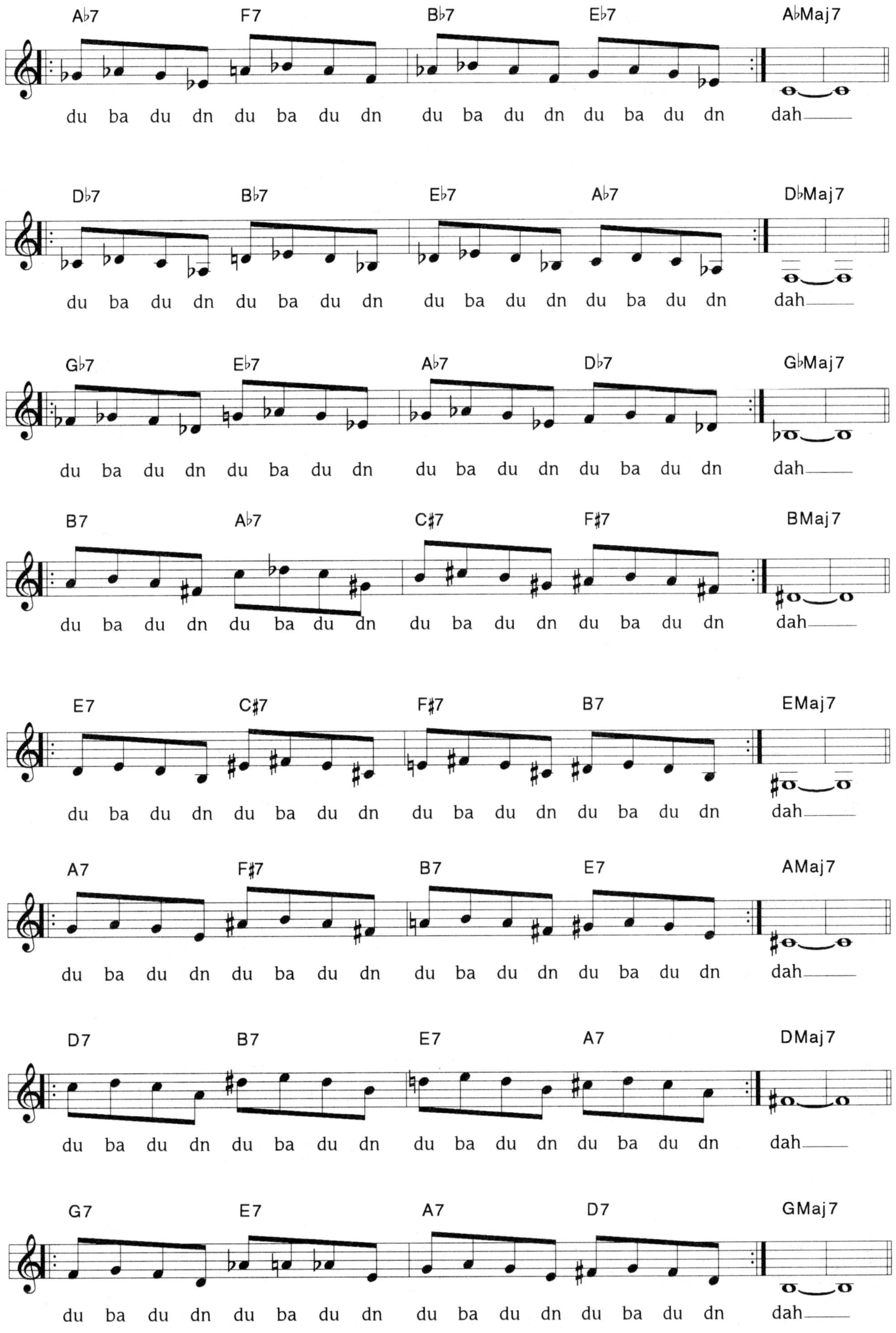

C7   A7   D7   G7   CMaj7

du ba du dn du ba du dn du ba du dn du ba du dn dah———

F7   D7   G7   C7   FMaj7

du ba du dn du dwe da ba du ba du dn du dwe da ba du dwe dah———

B♭7   G7   C7   F7   B♭Maj7

du ba du dn du dwe da ba du ba du dn du dwe da ba du dwe dah———

E♭7   C7   F7   B♭7   E♭Maj7

du ba du dn du dwe da ba du ba du dn du dwe da ba du dwe dah———

A♭7   F7   B♭7   E♭7   A♭Maj7

du ba du dn du dwe da ba du ba du dn du dwe da ba du dwe dah———

D♭7   B♭7   E♭7   A♭7   D♭Maj7

du ba du dn du dwe da ba du ba du dn du dwe da ba du dwe dah———

G♭7   E♭7   A♭7   D♭7   G♭Maj7

du ba du dn du dwe da ba du ba du dn du dwe da ba du dwe dah———

B7   A♭7   C♯7   F♯7   BMaj7

du ba du dn du dwe da ba du ba du dn du dwe da ba du dwe dah———

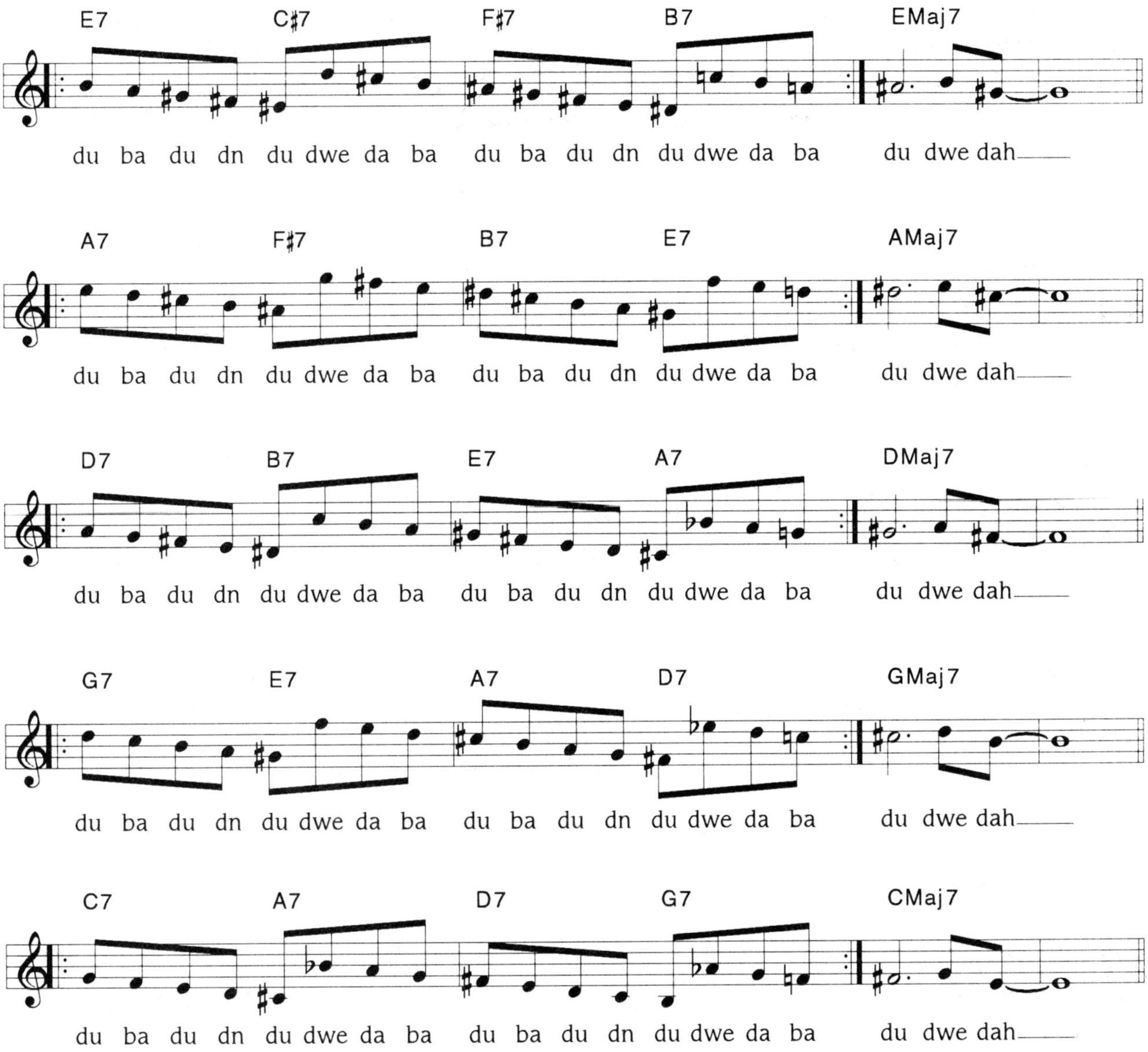

Locrian and Altered Mixolydian Scales

Swing feel

du dn du ba dwe ba du dn dwe du ba da dwe du dah____

du dn du ba dwe ba du dn dwe du ba da dwe du dah____

du dn du ba dwe ba du dn dwe du ba da dwe du dah____

du dn du ba dwe ba du dn dwe du ba da dwe du dah____

du dn du ba dwe ba du dn dwe du ba da dwe du dah____

du dn du ba dwe ba du dn dwe du ba da dwe du dah____

Eb-7b5   Ab7#9   3   C#min7

du dn du ba dwe ba du dn dwe du ba da dwe du dah___

C#-7b5   F#7#9   3   Bmin7

du dn du ba dwe ba du dn dwe du ba da dwe du dah___

B-7b5   E7#9   3   Amin7

du dn du ba dwe ba du dn dwe du ba da dwe du dah___

A-7b5   D7#9   3   Gmin7

du dn du ba dwe ba du dn dwe du ba da dwe du dah___

G-7b5   C7#9   3   Fmin7

du dn du ba dwe ba du dn dwe du ba da dwe du dah___

F-7b5   Bb7#9   3   Ebmin7

du dn du ba dwe ba du dn dwe du ba da dwe du dah___

Chapter 4: Melodic Solos

The following melodic solos demonstrate proper application of scat syllables, stylistic accents, melodic approaches, rhythmic embellishment, and harmonic considerations. Note how the melodic contour of each phrase consistently ascends and descends through the chord changes. Feel free to substitute your own spontaneous syllables whenever possible.

Blues in F

Swing feel

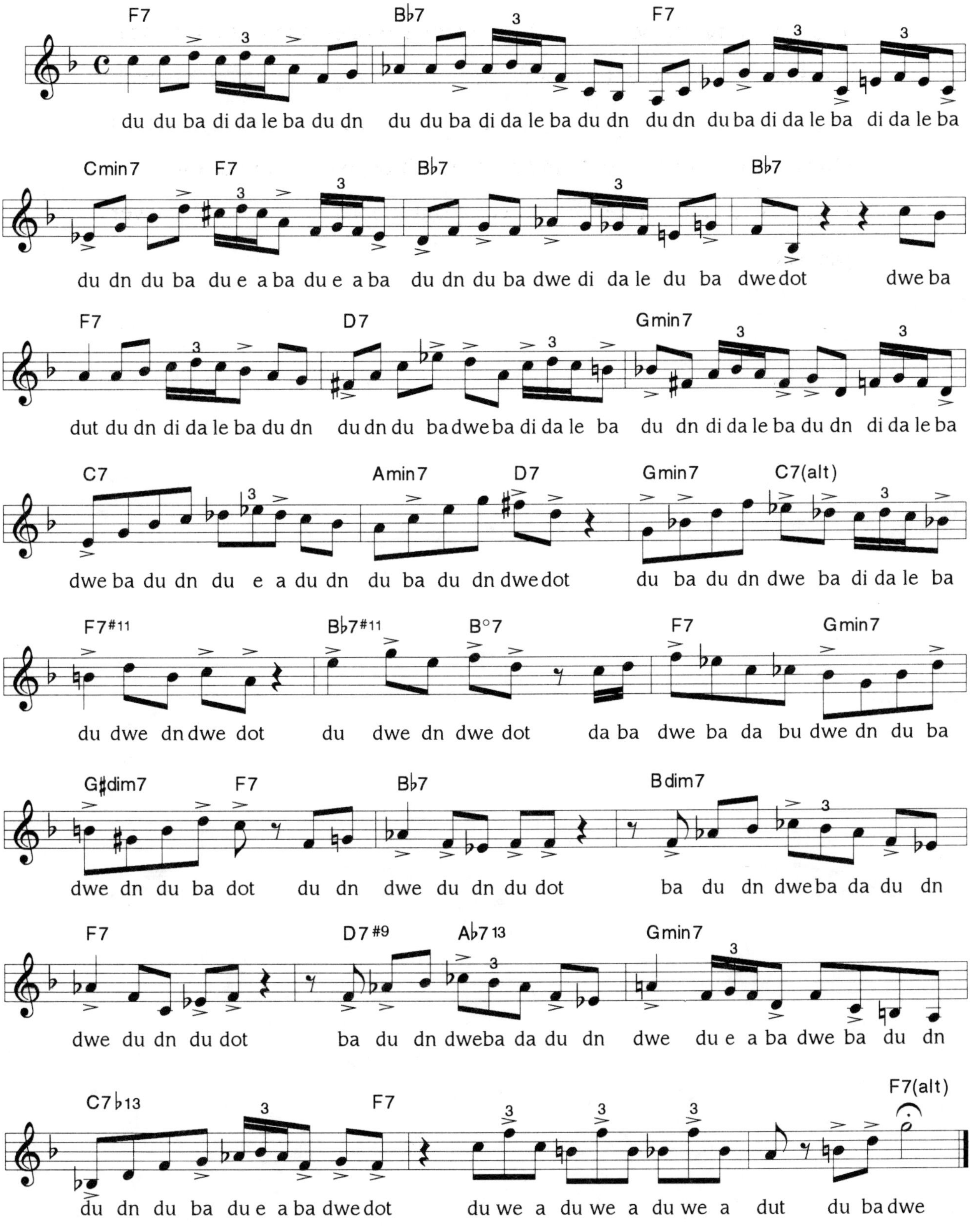

Minor 12 Bar Blues Solo

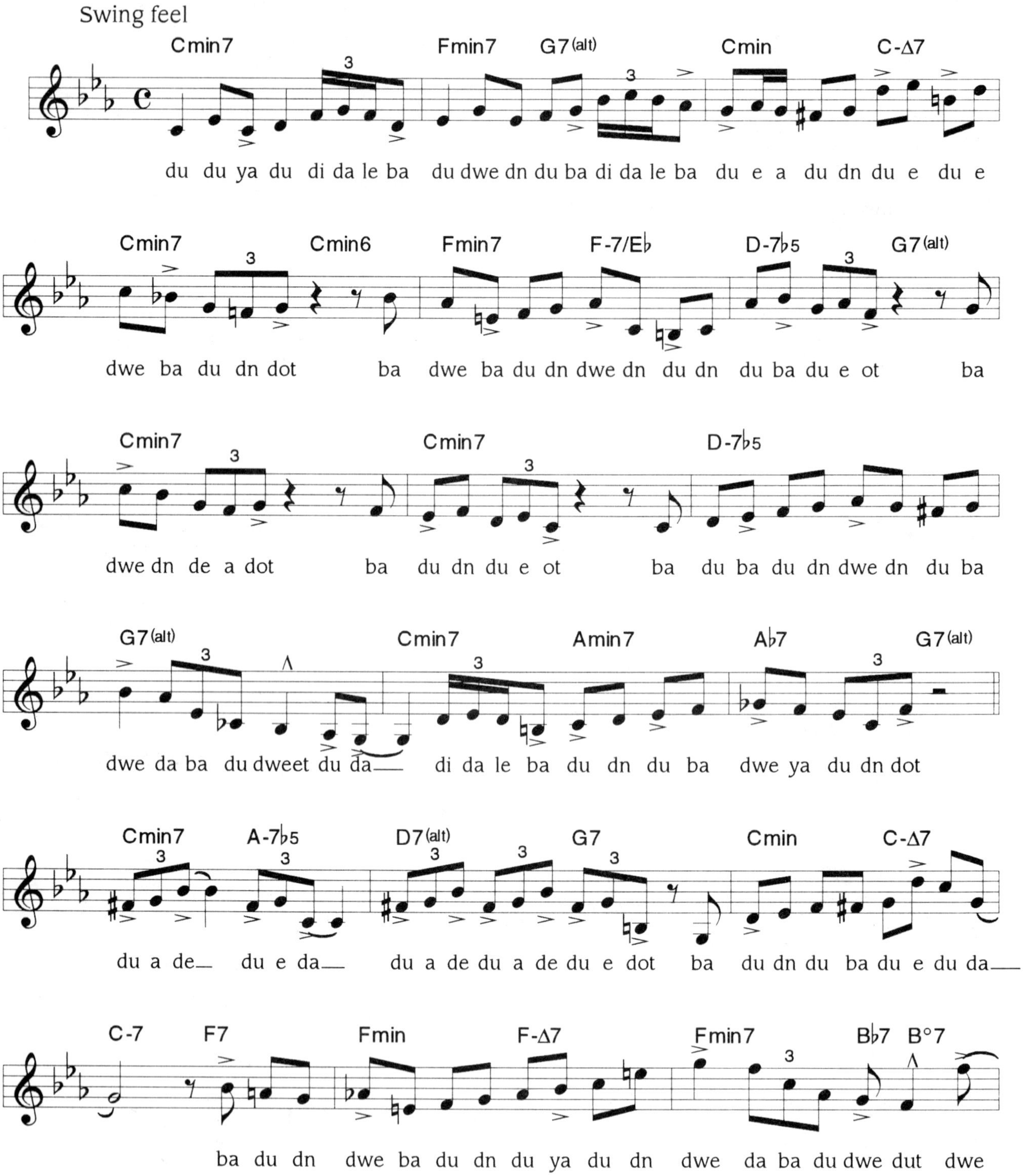

da ba du dwe di da lu da___   ba di da le ba du dn de a da___ ba

dwe ba du dn de a da___ ba de a da ba de a da ba di da la ba du dn dot

du ba du dn dwe dn du   dwe dn du du dn dwe___ ba da ba da du dwe du dah___

ba du ba di dl li dl du ba du dn de ba du dn di dl li dl

le ba du dn di dl a du dn di dl a di dl a di dl a du dn

de a da ba de a da ba de ba du dn de a da ba dot dwe___ da ba du dwe dot dwe___

da ba du dweet du dah___   ba dwe ba du dn du ya du wah___

Rhythm Changes Solo

di da le ba du dn du dn dwe ba dwe dn du ba di da le ba du dn du dn du ba dwe dot

du dn du ba di da le ba du dn du dwe ba dut dut du dwe ba di da le ba du dwe__

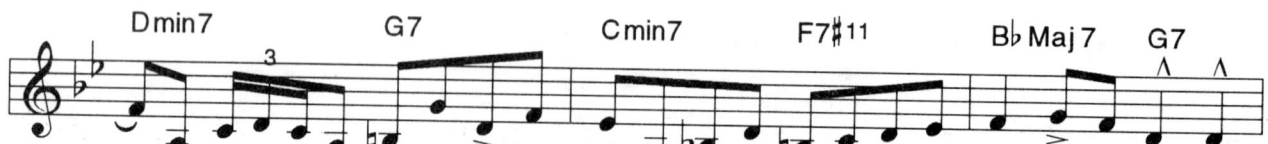

ba di da le ba du ba du dn dwe ba du dn du e du dn du dwe ba dut dut

di da le ba du dn du did dl lu du__ e a ba du dn du e dot ba

dwe ba du dn di da le ba du dn du ba du dn dwe dot

du dn du ba dwe ba du dn di da le ba di da le ba di da le ba dwe dot

D7 Amin7 D7♯11
3 3
dwe ba du dn du dn dwe ba di da lu di da lu de dut dwe
Dmin Dmin Δ7 Dmin7 G7 Gmin7
3 3 3 3
da ba du dwe ba da ba du dwe ba da ba du dwe dut da ba du dn di da le ba du dn
C7 C7♯11 Cmin7 F7♯11 Cmin7 F7
3 3 3
de ba du dn du de dut dwe dn du ba du dn dwe ba di da le ba di da le ba du dot
B♭Maj6 B○7 Cmin7 C♯○7 Dmin7 G7♯11
du du dn dwe da du du ba dwe ba du dn dwe ba du dwe ba
Cmin7 F7♯11 B♭7 B♭7/D E♭7 E○7
dwe ba du dn du ba dwe du dn du ba dwe dn du di da lu dot ba
Dmin7 G7♯9 Cmin7 B7 B♭7 (alt)
rit.
du dn du dwe ba du dn du dwe ba dwe ba du dwe

Miss June

Swing feel

F∆7   F#°7   G min7

dut du ba dwe ba du dn   du ba du we du dn du ba   dwe dn du ba de a du dn

C7   A min7   D min7

du be a dn dwe dow   ba du ba da dwe dn du ba   du we du we ot   du dn

G min7   C7 (alt)   F∆7

dwe ba du dn dwe dow   dwe ba du dn dwe da——   bu da ba da dwe ba du dn

F#°7   G min7   C7 (alt)

di da le di da lu di da le di da lu   dwe dn du ba dadwe dn du ba   dwe ba du dn di da le ba du dn

A min7   D min7   C min7

dah   ba du dn de dn de dn du we du ba   de dn de dn de ya da ba

F7   Bb∆7   Ab min7   Db7

de ba du dn dwe dow   du ba du e ya——   du ba du dn du ba du we de ba du dn da— ba dwe ba du dn da— ba dwe ba du we du dah— ba

du we du da— ba du dn dut de ya de ya du dn du we du da— da— ba bu

dot de ya de ya du da— du ba du dn du da— ba du da— ba du da—

ba du da ba du de ya du dah—— ba du dwe da ba du de dut dah———

How Hot the Sun

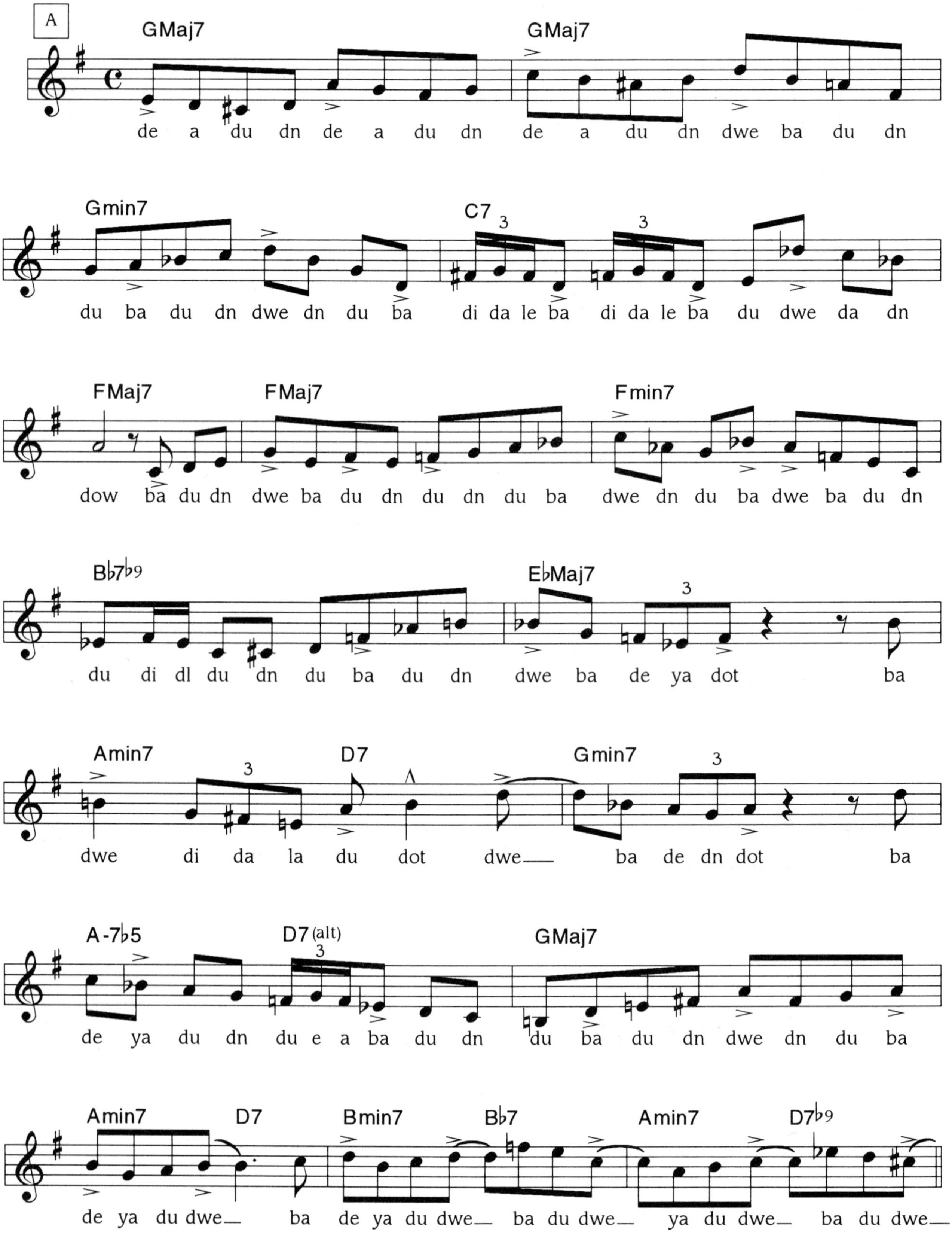

B
GMaj7 GMaj7
de ya dwe ba du dn di da le du dn dwe ba du dn
Gmin7 C7(alt)
dwe ba du dn du dn di da le ba dwe ba du dn du we yot
FMaj7 FMaj7
dot bu da dut dot dot bu da du
Fmin7 B♭7(alt)
ba de ba da du ya du dn dwe ba du dn du ba du dn
E♭Maj7 Amin7 D7♯11
dwe ba du dow ba du we du da du ba da
GMaj7 Amin7 D7
dwe ba du dow ba dwe ba du dn du dot dwe
Bmin7 B♭7 Amin7 D7
da ba du dwe dut dow ba da ba du de dot

C
GMaj7 GMaj7
dwe__ ba du dwe_ ba du dwe_ ba du dot dut ba
Gmin7 C7♯11 FMaj7
3
dwe dn du ba da du we du dow__ dwe dn du dot ba du dot
FMaj7 Fmin F–Δ7
3 3
ba du dn du ba dwe dn du ba di da le du ba di da le
Fmin7 B♭7 E♭Maj7
3 3 3
du ba di da le du dot ba du dn du we a ba du da la
Amin7 D7 Gmin7
3 3
dwe da ba du dwe dot dwe__ da ba du dwe da
A-7♭5 D7 (alt) GMaj7
3
ba du ba du dn di da le ba dut dwe dow__ ba
Amin7 D7 Bmin7 B♭7 Amin7 D7
du ba du dn du ba dwe dow________ ba du dot

D
GMaj7 GMaj7
ba du dot ba du ba du dn du ba dwe dut dow
Gmin7 C7(alt)
ba du ya dwe ba du dn de ya de ya de ya de ya
FMaj7 FMaj7
du we du dow ba du dn di da le du dn dwe ba du dn
Fmin7 B♭7(alt)
du dn du ba de ya du dn dwe ba du dn du ya du dn
E♭Maj7 Amin7 D7(alt)
dow ba da ba du dwe dn du ba du we a ba du dn
GMaj7 Amin7 D7
du di da le dow ba du di da le du ba du dwe
Bmin7 B♭7 Amin7 D7 GMaj7
ba du dwe ba dwe da ba du dwe dut dow

Chapter 5: Vocal Bass Lines

It is not difficult to imitate the acoustic bass. In terms of articulation, the syllable *doon* sounds most authentic when applied to the quarter note, particularly in jazz swing feel, and should resonate as fully as possible regardless of range. (Women should sing in their octave.) While this syllable works well for notes of longer duration, additional syllables may be added to phrases in which a note is preceded by triplet or dotted eighth–sixteenth (♩.♪) figures: *di-ga-ba doon* for triplets; *doon-ga doon* for dotted eight–sixteenth figures. Remember that in jazz swing feel the dotted eighth–sixteenth figure is interpreted as an eighth-note triplet. The syllable *ga* is sometimes written with percussion notation because on the bass it is played as a ghost note. Vocalists may sing these notes with or without pitch.

All of the following exercises move harmonically through the cycle of 5ths, each emphasizing different chord tones starting with the root and including the 3rd, 5th and 7th.

Cycle 5 Roots/5ths

Cycle 5 Roots/5ths/7ths

Cycle 5 Roots/3rds/7ths

Walking Bass Line 1

Two Walking Bass Lines

Walking Bass Line Theme and Variations

Theme

Variation 1

Swing feel

Variation 2

Swing feel

di ga ba dn dn ga dn   dn dn dn dn   di ga ba dn dn ga dn   dn dn dn dn

di ga ba dn dn ga dn   dn dn dn dn   di ga ba dn dn ga dn   dn dn dn dn

di ga ba dn dn ga dn   dn dn dn dn   di ga ba dn dn ga dn   dn dn dn dn

di ga ba dn dn ga dn   dn dn dn dn   di ga ba dn dn ga dn   dn dn dn dn

di ga ba dn dn ga dn   dn dn dn dn   di ga ba dn dn ga dn   dn dn dn dn

di ga ba dn dn ga dn   dn dn dn dn   di ga ba dn dn ga dn   dn dn dn dn

Blues Bass Line

Rhythm Changes For Vocal Bass

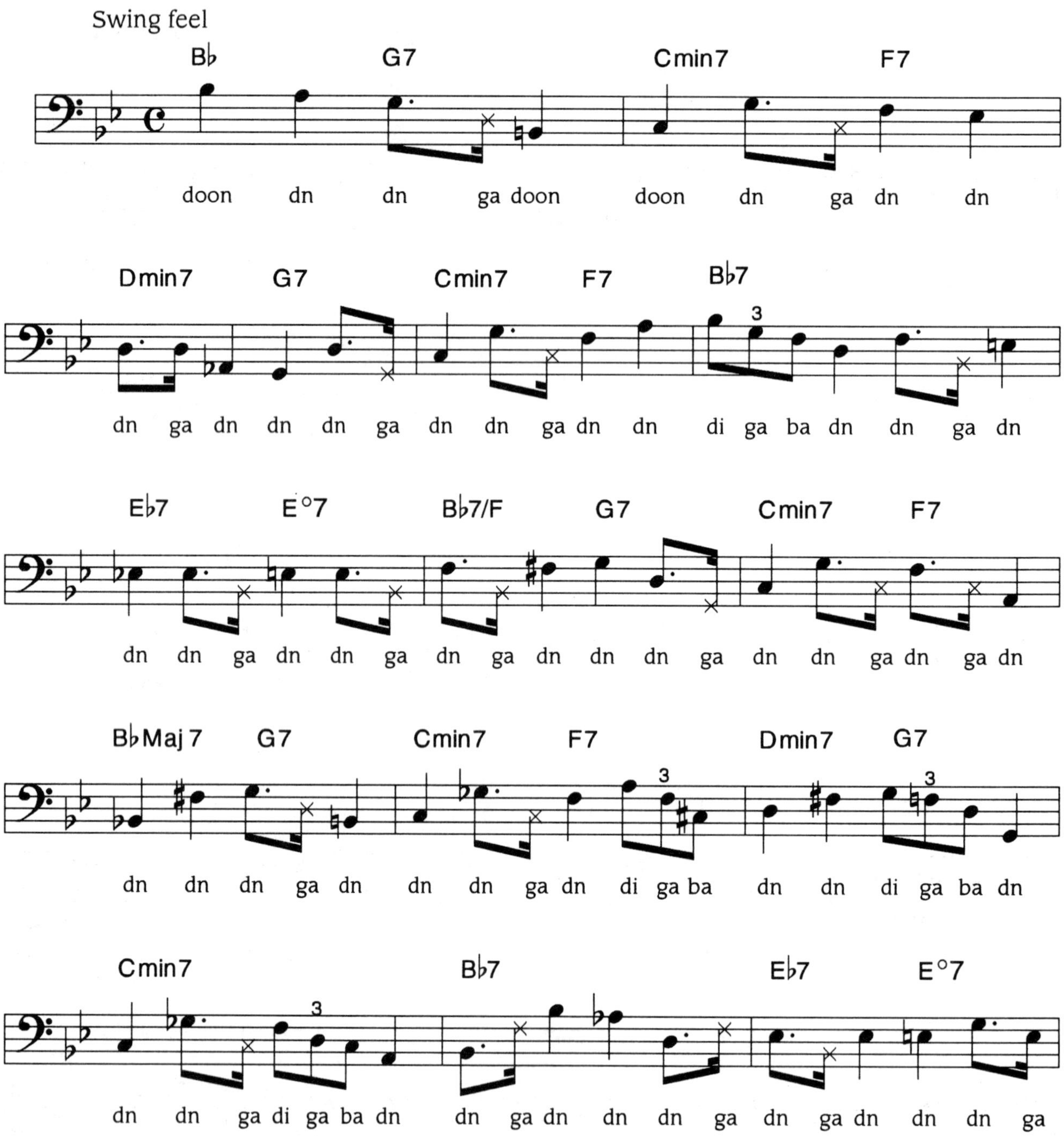

B♭/F B♭7 D7
dn dn dn ga dn dn ga dn dn dn dn dn ga dn dn
G7 D♭7
3
dn ga dn dn ga dn di ga ba dn dn ga dn dn dn dn ga dn
C7 F7
3
dn ga dn dn dn dn dn ga dn dn di ga ba dn dn ga dn
B♭ G7 C7 F7
3 3 3
dn dn dn ga dn di ga ba dn di ga ba dn dn dn ga di ga ba dn
D-7 A♭7 G7 D♭7 C-7 G♭7 F7 C♭7 B♭7
dn ga dn dn dn ga dn ga dn dn dn ga dn dn dn dn ga
E♭7 E°7 B♭7 F7 B♭7♯11
dn dn ga dn dn ga du dn dn dn du du du dut doon

Vocal Bass Fantasy

doon dn deen dn   doon dn deen dn   doon dn deen dn   doon dn deen dn   doon dn deen dn   doon   dn

Chapter 6: Vocal Drum Articulations

Contemporary scat singers frequently use percussive scat syllables to simulate drum beats, particularly in a cappella groups where there is no rhythm section to establish a groove. Stylistic drum grooves can easily be interpreted with a minimal vocabulary of syllables starting with the nucleus of the traditional trap set: bass drum, snare and hi hat. While bass and snare syllables are more consistent, a variety of articulations and timbres may be applied to cymbals, in particular, the hi hat. When pressed tightly together and played with a stick, the two hi-hat cymbals will make a staccato sound that can be vocalized with the single-letter syllable *t* (pronounced *tih*). Looser hi-hat cymbals can sound more like *tss* or *tsh* (pronounced *tiss* and *tish*). Other hi-hat sounds include *chik, tsik, tch, tsht* and so on. Additionally, there are numerous ride and crash cymbal syllables such as *ting, tang, psh* and *wsh*. Toms also may be articulated with the syllable *doon* with longer .duration and more variety of pitches from high to low. However for the purpose of establishing a groove, bass, snare and hi hat are sufficient.

Vocal Drum Articulations

Straight 8th Feel

Bass drum

doon doon doon doon   doon   dn dn   dn   dn dn   dn   dn dn   dn   dn dn dn   dn

dn   dn   dn   dn   dn   dn   dn dn   dn   dn dn   dn   dn   dn   dn   dn   dn dn

Bass drum and snare

doon ka doon ka   doon ka dn dn   ka   dn dn ka   dn dn ka   dn ka   dn ka dn

dn ka dn   ka   dn   ka dn   dn dn ka   dn   dn ka   dn   ka dn dn ka

Hi-hat

t   t   t   t   t t t   t t t   t t t t t t   t   t   t tss

tss t t tss t t   t t t tss t t   t   t t t tss t t   t tss

tsh   tsh   tsh t t tsh   tsh—it t tsh   tsh—it t tsh—it t

t t t t tsh—it t   t t tsh—it t tsh—it tsh—it tsh—it t tsh   tsh—it t tsh

Bass drum and hi-hat

(4)

dn t dn t dn t dn dn t dn t dn dn t dn dn t dn dn t

dn t t dn t dn t dn t dn dn t dn dn t dn t t t dn tsh

Snare and hi hat

(5)

ka t t ka t t ka t ka t ka t t ka t ka t ka t t ka t ka ka

tsh_ik ka tsh_ik ka t t ka t t ka tsh ka t t ka t t ka t ka t t ka tsh

Bass drum and snare with hi-hat

(6)

dn t t ka t t dn t ka t dn t t dn ka t t dn ka t t dn ka dn ka tsh

dn ka t ka dn ka t ka dn dn ka dn dn ka t ka t ka dn dn t ka dn dn dn ka t dn ka

dn t t dn ka t t dn dn t dn ka t dn ka t ka t ka t dn ka t dn ka t dn ka t dn ka t

ka t dn t ka dn t ka dn t ka dn t ka dn t ka t ka da t ka da t ka da dn tsh___

Vocal Drum Articulations

Triplet Feel

Hi-hat

t t t ts—it t t t t t ts—it t ts—it t t t t t

ts—it t t t t t t t t t ts—it t t tsh

t t t t ts—it t t t t t t t t t

t ts—it t t t t t t t tsh

Snare and hi-hat

ka t t ka t t ka t ka da t t ka t ka da t ka da t t ka t t

ka t ka t t ka da t ka t t ka t t ka t t ka t t ka dah

ka t t t t ka t t ka da t t ka t ka t ka t ka t ka da t t

ka da t ka da t ka t ka da da t ka t ka t ka t ka da t kah

Bass drum and hi-hat

doon t   t doon t   t   doon ts—it doon ts—it   dn t dn dn t dn   dn ts— it dn

dn t dn ts—it dn   dn t dn ts— it dn   ts—it dn ts—it dn   ts—it dn dn

t dn t   t dn t   dn t dn ts—it dn   t dn t   t dn t   t ts— it dn

dn ts— it t dn t   dn t ts—it dn t   dn dn t dn dn t   t dn dn dn

Bass drum and snare with hi-hat

dn t   t dn t   t ka t   t ka t   t   dn t   t ka t   t ka t   t dn

dn t dn ka t   t   ka t ka dn t   t   ka t dn ka t dn   ka t dn tsh

ka da dn t   t dn   ka da dn t   t dn   ka da dn ka da dn t   t dn ka

ka t ka t   t dn   ka t ka t   t dn   ka t   t ka t   t   ka t ka dn

108

Vocal Drum Articulations

16th Feel

Hi-hat

(1)

t t t t t t t t t t t t t ts‿it t t t t ts‿it t t t t t t t t t ts‿it t t t t ts——

it t t t t ts‿it ts‿it t t t t t t t t ts‿it t t t ts——it t t t t t t t t t t ts——

it ts‿it t t t t t t ts——it t t t t t t t t t tsh

Snare and Hi-hat

(2)

ka t t ka t t ka t t t t ka t t ka da t t t t ka tsh ka t t t ka t t t ka t t t t ka

t t ka t t ka t t ka da t t t ka t t t ka t t ka t t t ka da t t ka da t t ka da t t t ka

t ka t t t ka t t ka t ka t ka t t t t t ka t t t ka t t ka t t ka

Bass drum and hi-hat

③ dn t dn t dn t t t t dn t t dn dn t t t t t dn dn dn t t dn dn t t dn dn dn t t t dn

dn t t t dn dn t t t dn dn dn tsh t t t dn dn tsh t t t dn t dn t t dn t t t t dn tsh

dn tsh dn tsh t dn t dn dn tsh dn t t dn t t dn t dn t t dn tsh

Bass drum and snare with hi-hat

④ dn t t ka t t dn t t ka t t dn t t t ka t t t dn ka t t ka

dn ka t t dn ka t t dn ka t dn ka t t dn t t ka dn t t ka t t t ka dn

ka t t ka dn t t ka t t ka dn t t ka t t dn ka t t ka dn ka t t t

t t dn t ka t t t t t ka t dn t t ka t t ka da t t ka da t t ka dn

Shuffle Etude

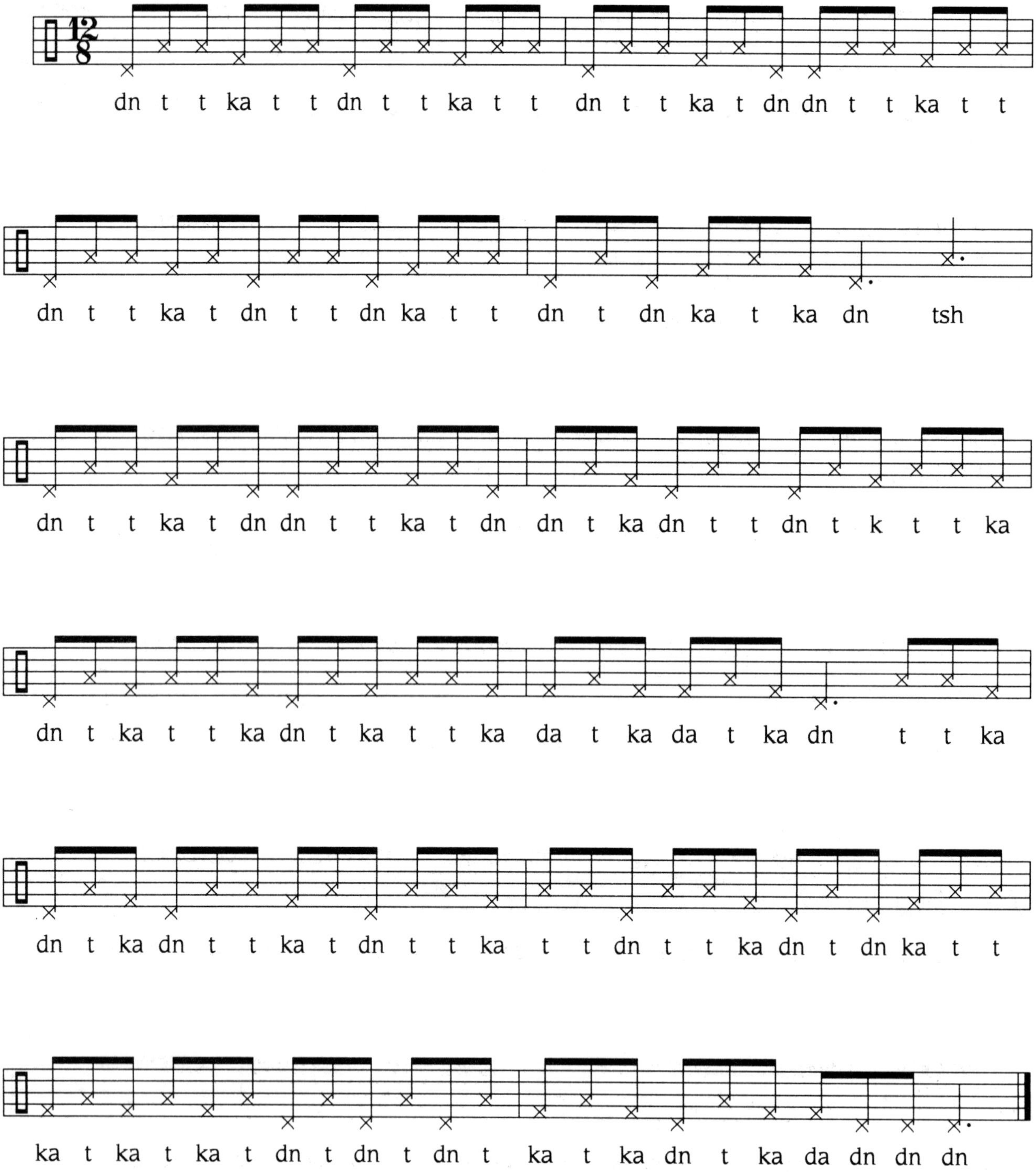

16th Funk Etude

doon t t ka t t dn t t ka t t   dn ka t t ka t t ka dn t t

ka t t dn ka t t dn ka t t   dn t t t t ka t t t ka dn

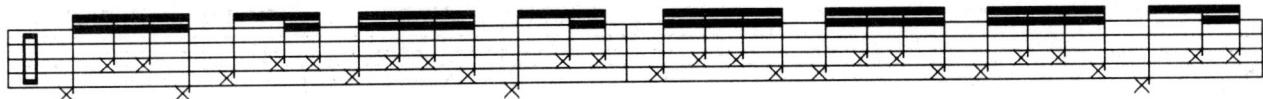

dn t t dn ka t t ka t t ka dn t t   ka t t ka da t t ka da t t ka dn t t

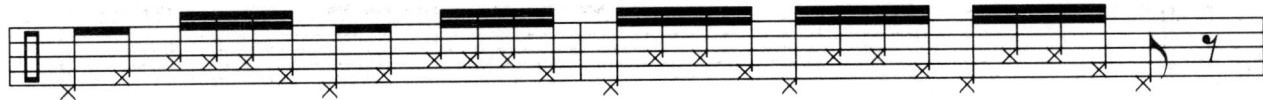

dn ka t t t ka dn ka t t t ka   dn t t ka dn t t ka dn t t ka dn

ka ts ka dn ka da ts ka da dn   ka da t t ka da t t ka da t ka dn

ka t t ka t t ka t t ka dn ka ts   ka t ka t ka da t ka t ka dn

Chapter 7: Solo A Cappella Technique

The most recent innovation in scat singing is solo a cappella technique, demonstrated in the early vocal works of Bobbie McFerrin. This style of vocal improvisation is exceptionally demanding on the performer who must provide all of the song's rhythmic, melodic and harmonic considerations with a single voice. This requires the skill to effectively simulate several musical instruments, as well as the ability to stylistically integrate them as one continuous line of music.

The following examples demonstrate solo a cappella technique in three different musical style feels: 1) Jazz blues, 2) Classical, and 3) R&B half time.

Solo A Cappella 12-Bar Blues

A Cappella Etude

Intro

dm dwe— ba du dwe du— du dm dwe— ba du dwe du dn du ba du dn

A

dm dwe— ba du dwe du— du dm dwe— ba du dwe du we du ma hwe oo dm ma du we

m bwe dee da dn du be du we du ma hwe oo du ma du dwe— bo bo bo ho bo bo bo oo we oo

du ma we oo dm hwe dm hwe dm hwe de de doh hoh hoo we oo

Interlude

du ma hwe du dm du be du dwe dm dwe— ba du dwe du— du

dm dwe— ba du dwe du dn du ba du dn dm dwe— ba du dwe du— du dm dwe— ba du dwe

B

dway boh doh day dm hm dway doh doh— day de de doh hm bwe dee doh hm dwe oo dm   bo ho bo bo bo ho bo bo bo ho bo bo   way boh doh day dm hm

dway   doh doh___ day   dee hee doh hm bwe de hm hm bwe day___

C

bo bo bo bo ho bo bo bo ho bo bo doh day   dm ma hwe doo dm ma du ee

dm bwe de da dn du be du way du ma hwe oo du ma du dwe___ bo bo bo ho bo bo bo oo we oo

du ma we oo dm hwe dm hwe dm hwe de de doh hoh hoo ee oo

dm ma hwe oo dm hwe dm hwe dm hwe de de doh hoh hoo ee oo dm ma hwe dah___ bah ba___

do ba ba ba do ba ba ba do ba ba ba do ba ba dm da ba dee da dm da ba du da

Repeat & Fade

dm dwe___ ba du dwe du___ du dm dwe___ ba du dwe du dn du ba du dn

Walkin'

16th feel

Sharon Broadley-Martin and Bob Stoloff

Vamp 1 G7 — C7

doon ga du-ba-di-dl li-di-dit dwe doon doon ga du-ba di-dl li-di dut did-a lee du-dee

Vamp 2 G7 — **1.** C7

doo ma did-a-lee wooh doom doo ma did-a-lee wooh wooh

2. C7 — **A** G7

doo ma did-a-lee 1.Don't mind walk-in' in the day-time don't mind
2.See the dif-frent kinds of peo-ple come from

C7 — G7

walk-in' in the night__ I don't mind walk-in' in-fact I like swing-in' from__
dif-frent frames of mind__ ev-er-y face goes a dif-r-nt place but they

C7 — G7

__ left to right___ I got a beat that's flow-in'
all move in time___ (The) girl with the Co-ca-Co-la

C7 — G7

mm I got a rhy-thm go-in' Dut du du dwe__ du-dn du du-dn
mm Well she's a Ho-ly Rol-ler

G7
Emin7
dwe du - dl lu lu dat
In the ci ty
mm Bus - y side walks on
C7
Emin7
an - y day du du du du
I tell the peo - ple that get
cit - y streets du du du du
And all I see there is
C7
D7
G
G/B
in my way that
shuf - flin' feet And
I need room a to move
D.C. & take 2nd verse
C
C♯dim7
NC
G
G/B
C
C♯dim7
and groove to moo - woo - woo-ove and groove to move and groove
Vamp and fade out
G7
C7
3
doon ga du-ba-di-dl li-di-dit dwe doon doon ga du-ba di-dl li-di dut did-a lee du-dee

Chapter Eight: Sing-Along Chord Patterns

Pattern 1

Bossa feel

A | CMaj7 | CMaj7 | CMaj7 | CMaj7 (8X)

B | Dmin7 | G7 | CMaj7 | CMaj7 (4X)

C | Dmin7 | G7 | CMaj7 | Amin7 (4X)

D | CMaj7 | Amin7 | Dmin7 | G7 (8X) | CMaj7

Pattern 2

Swing feel

Cmin7 (8X) | Fmin7 (8X) | Bbmin7 (8X) | Ebmin7 (8X)

Abmin7 (8X) | Dbmin7 (8X) | F#min7 (8X) | Bmin7 (8X)

Emin7 (8X) | Amin7 (8X) | Dmin7 (8X) | Gmin7 (8X) | Cmin7

Pattern 3

Bossa feel

A | D-7 G7 | C-7 F7 | Bb-7 Eb7 | Ab-7 Db7 | F#-7 B7 | E-7 A7 (4X)

Shuffle feel

B | D-7 G7 | C-7 F7 | Bb-7 Eb7 | Ab-7 Db7 | F#-7 B7 | E-7 A7 (4X)

C Bossa feel

D-7 | G7 | C-7 | F7 | Bb-7 | Eb7 | Ab-7 | Db7 | F#-7 | B7 | E-7 | A7 (4X) | Dmin7

Pattern 4

Swing feel

Dmin7 | G7 | Cmin7 | F7 | Bbmin7 | Eb7

Abmin7 | Db7 | F#min7 | B7 | Emin7 | A7 (7X) | Dmin7

Pattern 5

Hip-hop feel

Gmin7 | C7 | Fmin7 | Bb7 | Ebmin7 | Ab7

C#min7 | F#7 | Bmin7 | E7 | Amin7 | D7 (3X)

Pattern 6

Double-time samba feel

Dmin7 | G7 | Gmin7 | C7 | Cmin7 | F7

Fmin7 | Bb7 | Bbmin7 | Eb7 | Ebmin7 | Ab7

Abmin7 | Db7 | Dbmin7 | Gb7 | F#min7 | B7

Bmin7 | E7 | Emin7 | A7 | Amin7 | D7 | GMaj7

Sing-along Patterns #1-6: These tracks are prepared for open solos, trading phrases of any length (I recommend 2-bar and 4-bar phrases) and are excellent for classroom or private use.

2

Chapter Nine: Vocal Drum Grooves

Rhythm section grooves are currently too multifarious to define using abbreviated labels like jazz, pop, rock, funk, country or rhythm & blues. Although each idiom has its own stylistic flavor, contemporary music usually combines the elements of two or more idioms in any given song. The result is a hybrid style and there are many.

Rock, for example, doesn't mean much to a rhythm section about to lay down a groove. Rock can be interpreted as jazz-rock, pop-rock, country-rock, funk-rock, fusion-rock, hard-rock, soft-rock, acid-rock, Latin-rock, 12/8-rock or rock & roll! A shuffle beat is a little more specific but it can also be played with a jazz, rock, rhythm & blues or country feel. Even swing styles vary in the jazz, Latin and country idioms. To make stylistic interpretation even more confusing, there are additional rhythmic considerations called "feels" that will also effect the groove. Some examples of rhythmic "feels" include ballad, half-time, double-time, straight, syncopated, 2-beat and walking.

Some grooves have sustained the same rhythmic components for many years with only changes in their label. A perfect example is the "swunk" groove which originated in the 70's. This swing and funk hybrid may be described as a double-time shuffle feel with a heavy back-beat or as a half-time back-beat with a shuffle feel, depending on how it is counted. This popular beat has had several incarnations which include "crush-groove," "new Jack," " rhythm & blues half-time shuffle," "shuffle-rock," "funk-shuffle" and "hip-hop."

Regardless of their numerous labels, all grooves can be reduced to a specific pulse. The pulse refers to the subdivision of the quarter note (or the "beat"). There are only three used in jazz and popular music: 8th, 16th and triplet. "Feels" are used to describe how beat subdivisions are to be interpreted. "Straight 8th feel" means play with a even 8th note pulse while "swing 8th feel" means play as if the underlying pulse was a triplet for each quarter (also called "swing 8ths"). The only straight triplet feel I know of is 12/8 rock in which every beat is played with evenly accented triplets.

Vocal Drum Grooves

The following vocal drum beats include 8th, 16th and triplet pulse grooves with variations in kick drum, high-hat and snare patterns. Both the 8th and 16th patterns were recorded with a "straight feel" while the triplet grooves have a "swing feel." Note that 8th and 16th grooves may also be practiced with a "swing feel" if desired.

8th feel variations

① dn t ka t dn t ka t dn t ka t dn t ka t dn dn ka t dn t ka t dn dn ka t dn t ka t

dn t ka dn dn t ka t dn t ka dn dn t ka t dn t ka t dn dn ka t dn t ka t dn dn ka t

dn t ka t dn t ka dn dn t ka t dn t ka dn dn dn ka t dn dn ka t dn dn ka t dn dn ka t

dn t ka dn dn t ka dn dn t ka dn dn t ka dn dn dn ka dn dn t ka t dn dn ka dn dn t ka t

dn t ka t dn dn ka dn dn t ka t dn dn ka dn dn t ka dn dn dn ka t dn t ka dn dn dn ka t

dn dn ka t dn t ka dn dn dn ka t dn t ka dn dn t ka t t dn ka dn dn t ka t t dn ka dn

dn t t dn dooj t dn dn t t dn dooj t dn

16th feel variations

(2) dn t t t ka t t t dn dn t t t ka t t t dn t t t ka t t t dn dn t t t ka t t t

dn t t t ka t t t dn t t t ka t t dn dn t t t ka t t t dn t t t ka t t dn

dn t t dn ka t t t dn t t t ka t t t dn t t dn ka t t t dn t t t ka t t t

dn t t t ka t t t dn t t dn ka t t t dn t t t ka t t t dn t t dn ka t t t

dn t t dn ka t t t dn t t dn ka t t t dn t t dn ka t t t dn t t dn ka t t t

dn t t t ka t t dn dn t t t ka t t dn dn t t t ka t t dn dn t t t ka t t dn

dn t t dn ka t t dn dn t t t ka t t t dn t t dn ka t t t dn dn t t t ka t t t

dn t t t ka t t t dn t t dn ka t t t dn t t t ka t t t dn t t dn ka t t t

dn t t t ka t t t dn t t dn ka dn t t dn t t t ka t t t dn t t dn ka dn t t

dn t t t ka dn t t dn t t t ka t t t dn t t t ka dn t t dn t t t ka t t t

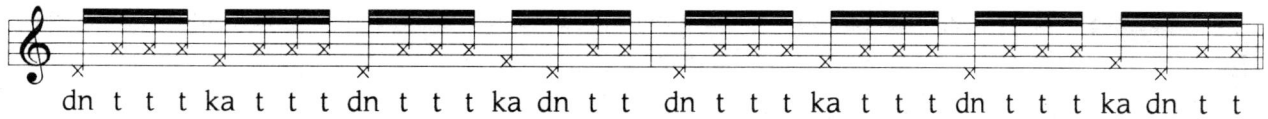

dn t t t ka t t t dn t t t ka dn t t dn t t t ka t t t dn t t t ka dn t t

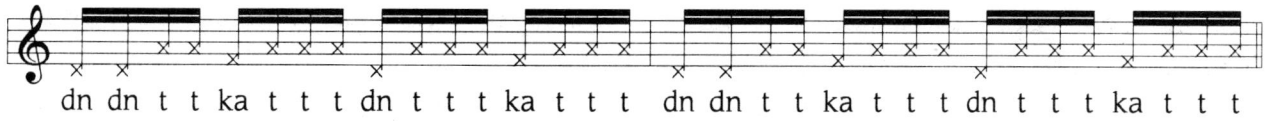

dn dn t t ka t t t dn t t t ka t t t dn dn t t ka t t t dn t t t ka t t t

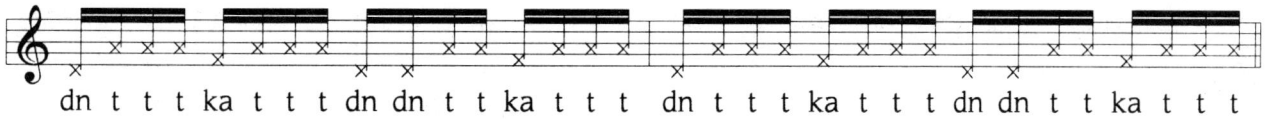

dn t t t ka t t t dn dn t t ka t t t dn t t t ka t t t dn dn t t ka t t t

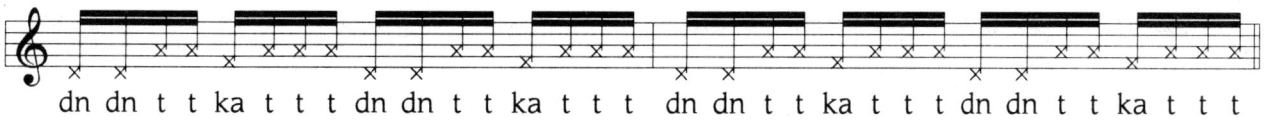

dn dn t t ka t t t dn dn t t ka t t t dn dn t t ka t t t dn dn t t ka t t t

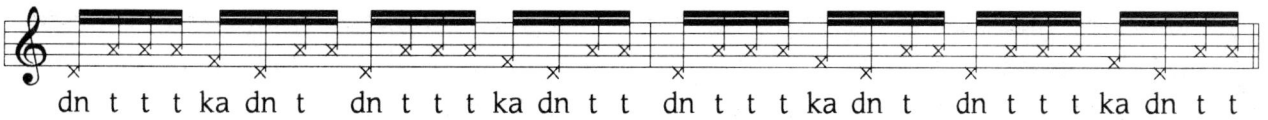

dn t t t ka dn t dn t t t ka dn t t dn t t t ka dn t dn t t t ka dn t t

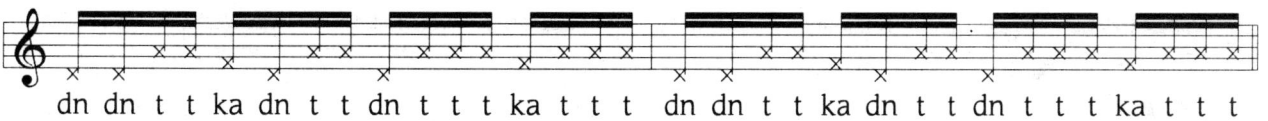

dn dn t t ka dn t t dn t t t ka t t t dn dn t t ka dn t t dn t t t ka t t t

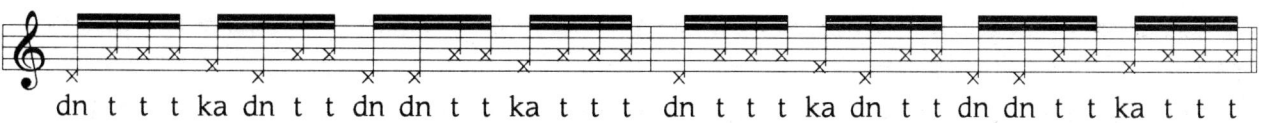

dn t t t ka dn t t dn dn t t ka t t t dn t t t ka dn t t dn dn t t ka t t t

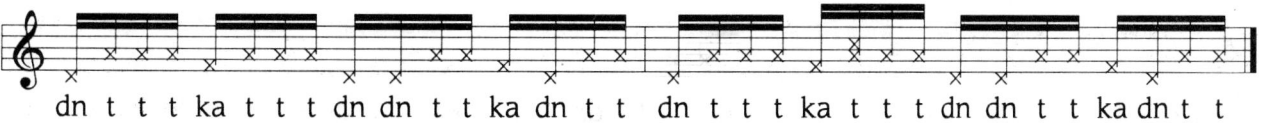

dn t t t ka t t t dn dn t t ka dn t t dn t t t ka t t t dn dn t t ka dn t t

More Syncopated Variations

③

dn t t t ka dn t dn dn t t ka t t t dn t t t ka dn t dn dn t t ka t t t dn t t t ka t t t dn t dn t ka dn t dn   dn t t t ka t t t dn t dn t ka dn t dn

dn t t t ka dn t dn dn t dn t ka t t t   dn t t t ka dn t dn dn t dn t ka t t t

dn t dn t ka dn t dn t ka dn t ka t t t   dn t dn t ka dn t dn t ka dn t ka t t t

dn t ka t t dn t t dn t t t ka t ts_it   dn t ka t t dn t t dn t t t ka t ts_it

dn t ka t t dn t dn t ka dn t ka t ts_it   dn t ka t t dn t dn t ka dn t ka t ts_it

dn t t ka t t t ka n t dn t ka t ts_it   dn t t ka t t t ka n t dn t ka t ts_it

dn t t ka t dn t ka dn t ts_it ka t ts_it   dn t t ka t dn t ka dn t ts_it ka t ts_it

dn t t ka t ka dn t t ka dn t ka t ts_it   dn t t ka t ka dn t t ka dn t ka t ts_it

dn t t ka t dn t dn t ka dn t ka t ts_it   dn t t ka t dn t dn t ka dn t ka t ts_it

dn t t dn t ka t dn dn t t ts_it ka t ts_it   dn t t dn t ka t dn dn t t ts_it ka t ts_it

Triplet Feel Grooves

Jazz swing with sticks

ting chik a ting chik a   ting chik a ting chik a   ting chik a ting chik a

Swing with brushes

ting chik a ting ka chik a   doof suf fa doof suf fa   doof suf fa doof suf fa

Swing Shuffle

doof suf fa doof suf fa   doof suf fa du fa su fa   ting ta ka ta ting ta ka ta

ting ta ka ta ting ta ka ta   ting ta ka ta ting ta ka ta   ting ta ka ta ting ta ka ta

Rock Shuffle

dn t ka t dn dn ka t   dn t ka t dn dn ka t   dn t ka t dn dn ka t

R&B half-time shuffle (hip-hop)

dn t ka t dn t t ka t dn   dn t t t ka t t dn dn t t t ka t t dn

dn t t t ka t t dn t t ka dn t ka t ts___it

Miscellaneous Grooves

Reggae

t t oon t t   t t oon ka da tsh   t t oon t t   t t oon ka dn tsh

Latin bossa nova

dn chik ka dn ka chi t ka ta chik ka dn ka chik ka

Latin samba

chik ka dn chik ka

ka chik ka dn chik ka

Afro-Cuban

dn dn t t ka dn dn dn dn dn dn t t ka dn dn dn dn

What's On the CD

1. Rhythm Etude #1 [p. 16]

2. Rhythm Etude #4 [p. 22]

3. Trad. Diatonic Pattern #5, Theme [p. 30]

4. Trad. Diatonic Pattern #5, Var. 1 [p. 30]

5. Trad. Diatonic Pattern #5, Var. 2 [p. 31]

6. Trad. Diatonic Pattern #5, Var.3 [p. 31]

7. Trad. Diatonic Pattern #6, straight [p. 32]

8. Trad. Diatonic Pattern #6, swing [p. 32]

9. Call-response Swing-A: This track begins with a 24-bar demo of a scat solo using non-pitched rhythmic phrases in the jazz swing style. 2-bar phrases follow with equivalent spaces for student response. Responses can be the same riff or your own creation.

10. Call-response Swing-B: This track is designed for trading 2-bar non-pitched scat syllable phrases right from the start.

11. Call-response Latin: Listen carefully to the Latin style interpretation of non-pitched scat sylables at the beginning of this track, then trade 2-bar phrases to the end.

12. Hammond B3 Blues: Four choruses of melodic scat over blues changes demonstrate stylistic accents, vowel placement and line contour. Two choruses of 2-bar trading follows for you to imitate riffs or create your own. The track winds down with five full choruses for open soloing.

13. Blues in F [p. 79]

14. 12-Bar Minor Blues [p. 80]

15. Rhythm Changes in Bb [p. 82]

16. Miss June [p. 84]

17. How Hot the Sun [p. 86]

18. Sing-along Pattern #1 [p. 118]

19. Sing-along Pattern #2 [p. 118]

20. Sing-along Pattern #3 [p. 118]

21. Sing-along Pattern #4 [p. 119]

22. Sing-along Pattern #5 [p. 119]

23. Sing-along Pattern #6 [p. 119]

24. Sing-along Pattern #7 [p. 76]

25. Sing-along Pattern #8 [p. 48]

26. Sing-along Pattern #9 [p. 50]

27. Sing-along Pattern #10 [p. 71]

28. Sing-along Pattern #11 [p. 70]

29. Shuffle Etude [p. 110]

30. 16th Funk Etude [p. 111]

31. Vocal Drum Grooves 1 [p. 121]

32. Vocal Drum Grooves 2 [p. 122]

33. Vocal Drum Grooves 3 [p. 124]

34. Vocal Drum Grooves 4 [p. 125]

35. Vocal Drum Grooves 5 [p. 126]

36. Vocal Drum Grooves 6 [p. 126]

37. Vocal Drum Grooves 7 [p. 126]

38. Vocal Drum Grooves 8 [p. 126]

39. Vocal Drum Call-Response: Listen to the opening 16-bar vocal drum solo,

then trade 2-bar phrases by imitating or creating your own drum riffs.

Musicians:
Brad Hatfield: Keyboards
John Chase: Drums
Bob Stoloff:Vocals

Instrumentals recorded at:
Brad Hatfield Productions, Westwood, Ma. Engineer: Brad Hatfield
John Chase Studio, Andover, MA. Engineer: John Chase
PBS, Westwood, MA. Engineer: Peter Kontrimas